Workshop on Frontiers in Linguistically Annotated Corpora 2006

Held in conjunction with COLING/ACL 2006

Sydney, Australia
22 July 2006

ISBN: 978-1-61738-512-4

Printed from e-media with permission by:

Curran Associates, Inc.
57 Morehouse Lane
Red Hook, NY 12571
www.proceedings.com

Some format issues inherent in the e-media version may also appear in this print version.

Printed by Curran Associates, Inc. (2010)

Association for Computational Linguistics
209 N. Eighth Street
Stroudsburg, Pennsylvania 18360

Phone: 1-570-476-8006
Fax: 1-570-476-0860

acl@aclweb.org

Table of Contents

Preface

Large linguistically interpreted corpora play an increasingly important role for machine learning, evaluation, psycholinguistics as well as theoretical linguistics. Many research groups are engaged in the creation of corpus resources annotated with morphological, syntactic, semantic, discourse and other linguistic information for a variety of languages. This workshop brings together researchers interested in the annotation of linguistically interpreted corpora by combining two workshops: Frontiers in Linguistic Annotation III and the 7th International Workshop on Linguistically Interpreted Corpora (LINC-2006). The goal of the workshop is to identify and disseminate best practice in the development and utilization of linguistically interpreted corpora.

We would like to thank all the authors who submitted papers. There were 19 submissions, of which 10 appear in the proceedings. We would like to particularly thank all the members of the program committee for their time and effort in ensuring that the papers were fairly assessed, and for the useful comments they provided.

In addition to regular papers, the workshop features presentations by working groups on two topics:

Annotation Compatibility: A roadmap of the compatibility of current annotation schemes with each other: *Annotation Compatibility Working Group Report.*

Low-density Languages: A discussion of low density languages and the problems associated with them: *Frontiers in Linguistic Annotation for Lower-Density Languages.*

The Innovative Student Annotation Award, for best paper by a student, went to Václav Novák, for his paper *On Distance between Deep Syntax and Semantic Representation.*

Organizers

Chairs:

Timothy Baldwin, University of Melbourne
Francis Bond, NTT Communication Science Laboratories
Adam Meyers, New York University
Shigeko Nariyama, University of Melbourne

Program Committee:

Lars Ahrenberg, Linköpings Universitet
Kathy Baker, U.S. Dept. of Defense
Steven Bird, University of Melbourne
Alex Chengyu Fang, City University Hong Kong
David Farwell, Computing Research Laboratory, New Mexico State University
Chuck Fillmore, International Computer Science Institute, Berkeley
Anette Frank, DFKI
John Fry, SRI International
Eva Hajicova, Center for Computational Linguistics, Charles University, Prague
Erhard W. Hinrichs, University of Tübingen
Ed Hovy, University of Southern California
Baden Hughes, University of Melbourne
Emi Izumi, NICT
Aravind Joshi, University of Pennsylvania, Philadelphia
Sergei Nirenburg, University of Maryland, Baltimore County
Stephan Oepen, University of Oslo
Boyan A. Onyshkevych, U.S. Dept. of Defense
Kyonghee Paik, KLI
Martha Palmer, University of Colorado
Manfred Pinkal, DFKI
Massimo Poesio, University of Essex
Owen Rambow, Columbia University
Peter Rossen Skadhauge, Copenhagen Business School
Beth Sundheim, SPAWAR Systems Center
Jia-Lin Tsai, Tung Nan Institute of Technology
Janyce Wiebe, University of Pittsburgh
Nianwen Xue, University of Pennsylvania

Working Group Organizers:

Adam Meyers, New York University
Mike Maxwell, University of Maryland

Workshop Program

Saturday, 22 July 2006

09:00–09:10	Opening Remarks
09:10–09:30	*Challenges for Annotating Images for Sense Disambiguation* Cecilia Ovesdotter Alm, Nicolas Loeff and David A. Forsyth
09:30–10:00	*A Semi-Automatic Method for Annotating a Biomedical Proposition Bank* Wen-Chi Chou, Richard Tzong-Han Tsai, Ying-Shan Su, Wei Ku, Ting-Yi Sung and Wen-Lian Hsu
10:00–10:30	*How and Where do People Fail with Time: Temporal Reference Mapping Annotation by Chinese and English Bilinguals* Yang Ye and Steven Abney
10.30–11.00	Coffee Break
11:00–11:30	*Probing the Space of Grammatical Variation: Induction of Cross-Lingual Grammatical Constraints from Treebanks* Felice Dell'Orletta, Alessandro Lenci, Simonetta Montemagni and Vito Pirrelli
11:30–12:00	*Frontiers in Linguistic Annotation for Lower-Density Languages* Mike Maxwell and Baden Hughes
12:00–12:30	*Annotation Compatibility Working Group Report* Adam Meyers
12:30–14.00	Lunch
14:00–14:30	*Manual Annotation of Opinion Categories in Meetings* Swapna Somasundaran, Janyce Wiebe, Paul Hoffmann and Diane Litman
14:30–15:00	*The Hinoki Sensebank — A Large-Scale Word Sense Tagged Corpus of Japanese —* Takaaki Tanaka, Francis Bond and Sanae Fujita
15:00–15:30	*Issues in Synchronizing the English Treebank and PropBank* Olga Babko-Malaya, Ann Bies, Ann Taylor, Szuting Yi, Martha Palmer, Mitch Marcus, Seth Kulick and Libin Shen
15.30–16.00	Coffee Break
16:00–16:30	*On Distance between Deep Syntax and Semantic Representation* Václav Novák
16.30–17.30	Discussion
17.30–17.40	Closing Remarks

Alternate papers

Corpus Annotation by Generation
Elke Teich, John A. Bateman and Richard Eckart

Constructing an English Valency Lexicon
Jiří Semecký and Silvie Cinková

Challenges for annotating images for sense disambiguation

Cecilia Ovesdotter Alm
Dept. of Linguistics
University of Illinois, UC
ebbaalm@uiuc.edu

Nicolas Loeff
Dept. of Computer Science
University of Illinois, UC
loeff@uiuc.edu

David A. Forsyth
Dept. of Computer Science
University of Illinois, UC
daf@uiuc.edu

Abstract

We describe an unusual data set of thousands of annotated images with interesting sense phenomena. Natural language image sense annotation involves increased semantic complexities compared to disambiguating word senses when annotating text. These issues are discussed and illustrated, including the distinction between word senses and iconographic senses.

1 Introduction

We describe a set of annotated images, each associated with a sense of a small set of words. Building this data set exposes important sense phenomena which not only involve natural language but also vision. The context of our work is *Image Sense Discrimination* (ISD), where the task is to assign one of several senses to a web image retrieved by an ambiguous keyword. A companion paper introduces the task, presents an unsupervised ISD model, drawing on web page text and image features, and shows experimental results (Loeff et al., 2006). The data was subject to single-annotator labeling, with verification judgements on a part of the data set as a step toward studying agreement. Besides a test bed for ISD, the data set may be applicable to e.g. multimodal word sense disambiguation and cross-language image retrieval. The issues discussed concern concepts, and involve insights into semantics, perception, and knowledge representation, while opening up a bridge for interdisciplinary work involving vision and NLP.

2 Related work

The complex relationship between annotations and images has been explored by the library community, who study management practices for image collections, and by the computer vision community, who would like to provide automated image retrieval tools and possibly learn object recognition methods.

Commercial picture collections are typically annotated by hand, e.g. (Enser, 1993; Armitage and Enser, 1997; Enser, 2000). Subtle phenomena can make this very difficult, and content vs. interpretation may differ; an image of the Eiffel tower could be annotated with *Paris* or even *love*, e.g. (Armitage and Enser, 1997), and the resulting annotations are hard to use, cf. (Markkula and Sormunen, 2000), or Enser's result that a specialized indexing language gives only a "blunt pointer to regions of the Hulton collections", (Enser, 1993), p. 35.

Users of image collections have been well studied. Important points for our purposes are: Users request images both by object kinds, and individual identities; users request images both by what they depict and by what they are about; and that text associated with images is extremely useful in practice, newspaper archivists indexing largely on captions (Markkula and Sormunen, 2000).

The computer vision community has studied methods to predict annotations from images, e.g. (Barnard et al., 2003; Jeon et al., 2003; Blei and Jordan, 2002). The annotations that are predicted most successfully tend to deal with materials whose identity can be determined without shape analysis, like *sky*, *sea* and the like. More complex annotations remain difficult. There is no current theory of word sense in this context, because in most current collections, words appear in the most common sense only. Sense is known to be important, and image information can disambiguate word senses (Barnard and Johnson, 2005).

Proceedings of the Workshop on Frontiers in Linguistically Annotated Corpora 2006, pages 1–4,
Sydney, July 2006.

Word (#Annot. images)	QueryTerms	Senses	Coverage	Examples of visual annotation cues
BASS (2881)	5: bass, bass guitar, bass instrument, bass fishing, sea bass	1. **fish**	35%	any fish, people holding catch
		2. **musical instrument**	28%	any bass-looking instrument, playing
		3. related: fish	10%	fishing (gear, boats, farms), rel. food, rel. charts/maps
		4. related: musical instrument	8%	speakers, accessories, works, chords, rel. music
		5. unrelated	12%	miscellaneous (above senses not applicable)
		6. people	7%	faces, crowds (above senses not applicable)
CRANE (2650)	5: crane, construction cranes, whooping crane, sandhill crane, origami cranes	1. **machine**	21%	machine crane, incl. panoramas
		2. **bird**	26%	crane bird or chick
		3. **origami**	4%	origami bird
		4. related: machine	11%	other machinery, construction, motor, steering, seat
		5. related: bird	11%	egg, other birds, wildlife, insects, hunting, rel. maps/charts
		6. related: origami	1%	origami shapes (stars, pigs), paper folding
		7. people	7%	faces, crowds (above senses not applicable)
		8. unrelated	18%	miscellaneous (above senses not applicable)
		9. **karate**	1%	martial arts
SQUASH (1948)	10: squash+: rules, butternut, vegetable, grow, game of, spaghetti, winter, types of, summer	1. **vegetable**	24%	squash vegetable
		2. **sport**	13%	people playing, court, equipment
		3. related:vegetable	31%	agriculture, food, plant, flower, insect, vegetables
		4. related:sport	6%	other sports, sports complex
		5. people	10%	faces, crowds (above senses not applicable)
		6. unrelated	16%	miscellaneous (above senses not applicable)

Table 1: Overview of annotated images for three ambiguous query terms, inspired by the WSD literature. For each term, the number of annotated images, the expanded query retrieval terms (taken terms from askjeeves.com), the senses, their distribution coverage, and rough sample annotation guidelines are provided, with core senses marked in bold.

(a) *machine* (b) *bird* (c) *origami* (d) *karate* (e) *rel. to a* (f) *rel. to b* (g) *rel. to c* (h) *people* (i) *unrel.*

Figure 1: CRANE images with clear senses: (a-d) *core* senses, (e-g) *related* senses, (h) *people* and (i) *unrelated*. Related senses are associated with the semantic field of a core sense, but the core sense is visually absent or undeterminable.

3 Data set

The data set has images retrieved from a web search engine. We deliberately focused on three keywords, which cover a range of phenomena in semantic ambiguity: BASS, CRANE, and SQUASH. Table 1 gives an overview of the data set, annotated by one author (CA).[1] The webpage was not considered to avoid bias, given the ISD task.

For each query, 2 to 4 core word senses were distinguished from inspecting the data using common sense. We chose this approach rather than ontology senses which tend to be incomplete or too specific for our purposes. For example, the *origami* sense of CRANE is not included in WordNet under CRANE, but for BASS three different senses appear with fish. WordNet contains *bird* as part of the description for the separate entry *origami*, and some query expansion terms are hyponyms which occur as separate WordNet entries (e.g. *bass guitar*, *sea bass*, *summer squash*). Images may show multiple objects; a general strategy preferred a core sense if it was included.

An additional complication is that given that the images are retrieved by a search engine there is no guarantee that they depict the query term, so additional senses were introduced. Thus, for most core senses, a RELATED label was included for meanings related to the semantic field of a core sense. Also, a PEOPLE label was included since such images may occur due to how people take pictures (e.g. portraits of persons, group pictures, or other representations of people outside core and related senses). An UNRELATED label accounted for images that did not fit other labels, or were irrelevant or undeterminable. In fact, distinguishing between PEOPLE and UNRELATED was not always straightforward. Fig. 1 shows examples of CRANE when sense assignment was quite straightforward. However, distinguishing image senses was often not this clear. In fact, many border-line cases occurred when one could argue for different label assignments. Also, annotation cues are subject to interpretation, and disagreements between judges are expected. They simply reflect that image senses are located on a semantic continuum.

4 Why annotating image senses is hard

In general, annotating images involves special challenges, such as what to annotate and how extensively. We assign an image one sense. Nevertheless, compared to disambiguating a word, several issues are added for annotation. As noted above, a core sense may not occur, and judgements are characterized by increased subjectivity, with semantics beyond prototypical and peripheral

[1]We call the data set the *UIUC-ISD data set*. It is currently at http://www.visionpc.cs.uiuc.edu/isd/.

Figure 2: Annotating images is often challenging for different reasons. Are these images of CRANE birds? (a-c) depiction (d-f) gradient change (g-h) partial display (i-j) domain knowledge (k) unusual appearance (l-n) distance (o-q) not animate.

exemplars. Also, the disambiguating context is limited to image contents, rather than collocations of an ambiguous token. Fig. 2 illustrates selected challenging judgement calls for assigning or not the bird sense of CRANE, as discussed below.

Depiction: Images may include man-made depictions of an object in artistic depictions, and the question is whether this counts as the object or not, e.g. Fig. 2(a-c). **Gradient changes:** Recognition is complicated by objects taking different forms and shapes, cf. the insight by (Labov, 1973) on gradual categories.[2] For example, as seen in Fig. 2(d-f), birds change with age; an egg may be a bird, but a chick is, as is a fledgeling. **Partial display:** Objects may be rendered in incomplete condition. For example, Fig. 2(g-h) show merely feathers or a bird neck. **Domain knowledge:** People may disagree due to differences in domain knowledge, e.g. some non-experts may have a difficult time determining whether or not other similar bird species can be distinguished from a bird crane, cf. Fig. 2(i-j). This also affected annotations' granularity depending on keyword, see Table 1's example cues. **Unusual appearance:** Objects may occur in less frequent visual appearance, or lack distinguishing properties. For instance, Fig. 2(k) illustrates how sunset background masks birds' color information. **Scale:** The distance to objects may render them unclear and influence judgement accuracy, and people may differ in the degree of certainty required for assigning a sense. For example, Fig. 2(l-n) show flying or standing potential cranes at distance. **Animate:** Fig. 2(o-q) raise the question whether dead, skeletal, or artificial objects are instantiations or not. Other factors complicating the annotation task include image **crowdedness** disguising objects, certain entities having less **salience**, and lacking or unclear **reference to object proportions**. Senses may also be **etymologically** related or **blend** occasionally, or be guided by **cultural** interpretations, and so on.

Moreover, related senses are meant to capture images associated with the semantic field of a core sense. However, because the notion and borders of a semantic field are non-specific, **related senses are tricky**. Annotators may build associations quite wildly, based on personal experience and opinion, thus what is or is not a related sense may very quickly get out of hand. For instance, a person may by association reason that if bird cranes occur frequently in fields, then an image of a field alone should be marked as related. To avoid this, guidelines attempted to restrict related senses, as exemplified in Table 1, with some data-driven revisions during the annotation process. However, guidelines are also based on judgement calls. Besides, for abstract concepts like LOVE, differentiating core versus related sense is not really valid.

Lastly, an additional complexity of image senses is that in addition to traditional word senses, images may also capture repeatedly occurring **iconographic** patterns or senses. As illustrated in Fig. 3, the iconography of flying cranes is quite different from that of standing cranes, as regards motion, shape, identity, and color of figure and ground, respectively. Mixed cases also occur, e.g. when bird cranes are taking off or are about to land in relation to flight. Iconographic senses may compare to more complex linguistic structures than nominal categories, e.g. a modified NP or clause, but are represented by image properties.

A policy for annotating iconographic senses is still lacking. Image groups based on iconographic senses seem to provide increased visual and semantic harmony for the eye, but experiments are needed to confirm how iconographic senses correspond to humans' perception of semantic image similarity, and at what level of semantic differen-

[2]Function or properties may also influence (Labov, 1973).

(a) (b) (c) (d) (e) (f) (g) (h)

Figure 3: Iconographic bird CRANE senses: (a-c) *flying cranes*, (d-f) *standing cranes*, and (g-h) *mixed cases* in-between.

(a) 5/2 (b) 1/4 (c) 4/1 (d) 4/1 (e) 4/8 (f) 8/2 (g) 8/1 (h) 6/8,5 (i) 4/1

Figure 4: Disagreement examples (sense numbers in Table 1): (a) crane or other bird? (b) toy crane or scales? (c) crane or other steel structure/elevator? (d) crane or other machine? (e) company is related or not? (f) bird or abstract art? (g) crane in background or not? (h) origami-related paper? (i) inside of crane? (and is inside sufficient to denote image as machine crane?)

tiation they become relevant for sense assessment.

Lastly, considering the challenges of image annotation, it is interesting to look at annotation disagreements. Thus, another author (NL) inspected CRANE annotations, and recorded disagreement candidates, which amounted to 5%. Rejecting or accepting a category label seems less hard than independent annotation but still can give insights into disagreement tendencies. Several disagreements involved a core category vs. its related label vs. unrelated, rather than two core senses. Also, some disagreement candidates had tiny, fuzzy, partial or peripheral potential sense objects, or lacked distinguishing object features, so interpretation became quite idiosyncratic. The disagreement candidates were discussed together, resulting in 2% being true disagreements, 2% false disagreements (resolved by consensus on CA's labels), and 1% annotation mistakes. Examples of true disagreements are in Fig. 4. Often, both parties could see each others' points, but opted for another interpretation; this confirms that border lines tend to merge, indicating that consistency is challenging and not always guaranteed. As the annotation procedure advances, criteria may evolve and modify the fuzzy sense boundaries.

5 Conclusion

This work draws attention to the need for considering natural language semantics in multi-modal settings. Annotating image senses adds increased complexity compared to word-sense annotation in text due to factors such as image properties, subjective perception, and annotator domain-knowledge. Moreover, the concept of related senses as well as iconographic senses go beyond and diversify the notion of word sense. In the future, we would like to perform experimentation with human subjects to explore both similarity judgements for image pairs or groups, as well as issues in interannotator agreement for image disambiguation, and, finally, to better understand the role of iconography for semantic interpretation.

6 Acknowledgements

Thanks to anonymous reviewers, R. Girju and R. Sproat for feedback. Any fallacies are our own.

References

L. H. Armitage and P. G. B. Enser. 1997. Analysis of user need in image archives. *J. of Inform. Sci.*, 23(4):287–299.

K. Barnard and M. Johnson. 2005. Word sense disambiguation with pictures. *Artif. Intel.*, 167:13–30.

K. Barnard, P. Duygulu, N. Freitas, D. Forsyth, D. Blei, and M. I. Jordan. 2003. Matching words and pictures. *J. of Mach. Learn. Research*, 3:1107–1135.

D. M. Blei and M. I. Jordan. 2002. Modeling annotated data. Technical Report CSD-02-1202, Div. of Computer Science, Univ. of California, Berkeley.

P. G. B. Enser. 1993. Query analysis in a visual information retrieval context. *J. of Doc. and Text Management*, 1(1):25–52.

P. G. B. Enser. 2000. Visual image retrieval: seeking the alliance of concept based and content based paradigms. *J. of Inform. Sci.*, 26(4):199–210.

J. Jeon, V. Lavrenko, and R. Manmatha. 2003. Automatic image annotation and retrieval using crossmedia relevance models. In *SIGIR*, pages 119–126.

W. Labov. 1973. The boundaries of words and their meanings. In C. J. Baily and R. Shuy, editors, *New ways of analyzing variation in English*, pages 340–373. Washington D.C: Georgetown Univ. Press.

N. Loeff, C. O. Alm, and D. A. Forsyth. 2006. Discriminating image senses by clustering with multimodal features. In *ACL (forthcoming)*.

M. Markkula and E. Sormunen. 2000. End-user searching challenges indexing practices in the digital newspaper photo archive. *Inform. Retr.*, 1:259–285.

A Semi-Automatic Method for Annotating a Biomedical Proposition Bank

Wen-Chi Chou[1], Richard Tzong-Han Tsai[1,2], Ying-Shan Su[1], Wei Ku[1,3], Ting-Yi Sung[1] and Wen-Lian Hsu[1]

[1]Institute of Information Science, Academia Sinica, Taiwan, ROC.

[2]Dept. of Computer Science and Information Engineering, National Taiwan University, Taiwan, ROC.

[3]Institute of Molecular Medicine, National Taiwan University, Taiwan, ROC.

{jacky957,thtsai,qnn,wilmaku,tsung,hsu}@iis.sinica.edu.tw

Abstract

In this paper, we present a semi-automatic approach for annotating semantic information in biomedical texts. The information is used to construct a biomedical proposition bank called BioProp. Like PropBank in the newswire domain, BioProp contains annotations of predicate argument structures and semantic roles in a treebank schema. To construct BioProp, a semantic role labeling (SRL) system trained on PropBank is used to annotate BioProp. Incorrect tagging results are then corrected by human annotators. To suit the needs in the biomedical domain, we modify the PropBank annotation guidelines and characterize semantic roles as components of biological events. The method can substantially reduce annotation efforts, and we introduce a measure of an upper bound for the saving of annotation efforts. Thus far, the method has been applied experimentally to a 4,389-sentence treebank corpus for the construction of BioProp. Inter-annotator agreement measured by kappa statistic reaches .95 for combined decision of role identification and classification when all argument labels are considered. In addition, we show that, when trained on BioProp, our biomedical SRL system called BIOSMILE achieves an F-score of 87%.

1 Introduction

The volume of biomedical literature available on the Web has grown enormously in recent years, a trend that will probably continue indefinitely. Thus, the ability to process literature automatically would be invaluable for both the design and interpretation of large-scale experiments. To this end, several information extraction (IE) systems using natural language processing techniques have been developed for use in the biomedical field. Currently, the focus of IE is shifting from the extraction of nominal information, such as named entities (NEs) to verbal information that represents the relations between NEs, e.g., events and function (Tateisi et al., 2004; Wattarujeekrit et al., 2004). In the IE of relations, the roles of NEs participating in a relation must be identified along with a verb of interest. This task involves identifying main roles, such as agents and objects, and adjunct roles (ArgM), such as location, manner, timing, condition, and extent. This identification task is called *semantic role labeling* (SRL). The corresponding roles of the verb (*predicate*) are called *predicate arguments*, and the whole proposition is known as a *predicate argument structure* (PAS).

To develop an automatic SRL system for the biomedical domain, it is necessary to train the system with an annotated corpus, called *proposition bank* (Palmer et al., 2005). This corpus contains annotations of semantic PAS's superimposed on the Penn Treebank (PTB) (Marcus et al., 1993; Marcus et al., 1994). However, the process of manually annotating the PAS's to construct a proposition bank is quite time-consuming. In addition, due to the complexity of proposition bank annotation, inconsistent annotation may occur frequently and further complicate

Proceedings of the Workshop on Frontiers in Linguistically Annotated Corpora 2006, pages 5–12,
Sydney, July 2006.

the annotation task. In spite of the above difficulties, there are proposition banks in the newswire domain that are adequate for training SRL systems (Xue and Palmer, 2004; Palmer et al., 2005). In addition, according to the CoNLL-2005 shared task (Carreras and Màrquez, 2005), the performance of SRL systems in general does not decline significantly when tagging out-of-domain corpora. For example, when SRL systems trained on the Wall Street Journal (WSJ) corpus were used to tag the Brown corpus, the performance only dropped by 15%, on average. In comparison to annotating from scratch, annotation efforts based on the results of an available SRL system are much reduced. Thus, we plan to use a newswire SRL system to tag a biomedical corpus and then manually revise the tagging results. This semi-automatic procedure could expedite the construction of a biomedical proposition bank for use in training a biomedical SRL system in the future.

2 The Biomedical Proposition Bank - BioProp

As proposition banks are semantically annotated versions of a Penn-style treebank, they provide consistent semantic role labels across different syntactic realizations of the same verb. The annotation captures predicate-argument structures based on the sense tags of polysemous verbs (called *framesets*) and semantic role labels for each argument of the verb. Figure 1 shows the annotation of semantic roles, exemplified by the following sentence: "IL4 and IL13 receptors activate STAT6, STAT3 and STAT5 proteins in normal human B cells." The chosen predicate is the word "activate"; its arguments and their associated word groups are illustrated in the figure.

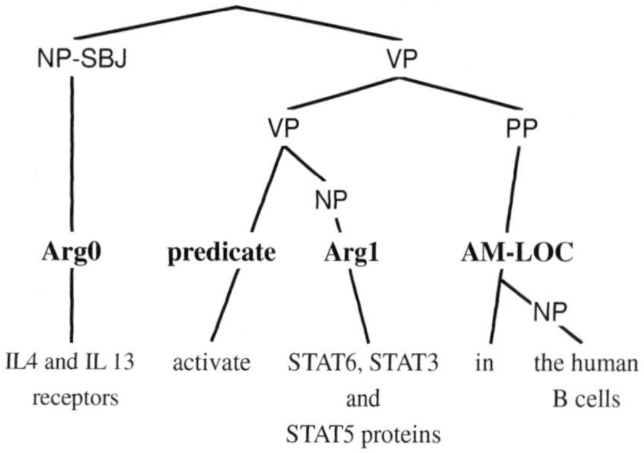

Figure 1. A treebank annotated with semantic role labels

Since proposition banks are annotated on top of a Penn-style treebank, we selected a biomedical corpus that has a Penn-style treebank as our corpus. We chose the GENIA corpus (Kim et al., 2003), a collection of MEDLINE abstracts selected from the search results with the following keywords: human, blood cells, and transcription factors. In the GENIA corpus, the abstracts are encoded in XML format, where each abstract also contains a MEDLINE UID, and the title and content of the abstract. The text of the title and content is segmented into sentences, in which biological terms are annotated with their semantic classes. The GENIA corpus is also annotated with part-of-speech (POS) tags (Tateisi and Tsujii, 2004), and co-references are added to part of the GENIA corpus by the MedCo project at the Institute for Infocomm Research, Singapore (Yang et al., 2004).

The Penn-style treebank for GENIA, created by Tateisi et al. (2005), currently contains 500 abstracts. The annotation scheme of the GENIA Treebank (GTB), which basically follows the Penn Treebank II (PTB) scheme (Bies et al., 1995), is encoded in XML. However, in contrast to the WSJ corpus, GENIA lacks a proposition bank. We therefore use its 500 abstracts with GTB as our corpus. To develop our biomedical proposition bank, BioProp, we add the proposition bank annotation on top of the GTB annotation.

In the following, we report on the selection of biomedical verbs, and explain the difference between their meaning in PropBank (Palmer et al., 2005), developed by the University of Pennsylvania, and their meaning in BioProp (a biomedical proposition bank). We then introduce BioProp's annotation scheme, including how we modify a verb's framesets and how we define framesets for biomedical verbs not defined in VerbNet (Kipper et al., 2000; Kipper et al., 2002).

2.1 Selection of Biomedical Verbs

We selected 30 verbs according to their frequency of use or importance in biomedical texts. Since our targets in IE are the relations of NEs, only sentences containing protein or gene names are used to count each verb's frequency. Verbs that have general usage are filtered out in order to ensure the focus is on biomedical verbs. Some verbs that do not have a high frequency, but play important roles in describing biomedical relations, such as "phosphorylate" and "transactivate", are also selected. The selected verbs are listed in Table 1.

Predicate	Frameset	Example
express (VerbNet)	**Arg0:** agent **Arg1:** theme **Arg2:** recipient or destination	[Some legislators$_{Arg0}$][expressed$_{predicate}$] [concern that a gas-tax increase would take too long and possibly damage chances of a major gas-tax-increasing ballot initiative that voters will consider next June$_{Arg1}$].
translate (VerbNet)	**Arg0:** causer of transformation **Arg1:** thing changing **Arg2:** end state **Arg3:** start state	But some cosmetics-industry executives wonder whether [techniques honed in packaged goods$_{Arg1}$] [will$_{AM\text{-}MOD}$] [translate$_{predicate}$] [to the cosmetics business$_{Arg2}$].
express (BioProp)	**Arg0:** causer of expression **Arg1:** thing expressing	[B lymphocytes and macrophages$_{Arg0}$] [express$_{predicate}$] [closely related immunoglobulin G (IgG) Fc receptors (Fc gamma RII) that differ only in the structures of their cytoplasmic domains$_{Arg1}$].

Table 2. Framesets and examples of "express" and "translate"

Type	Verb list
1	encode, interact, phosphorylate, transactivate
2	express, modulate
3	bind
4	activate, affect, alter, associate, block, decrease differentiate, encode, enhance, increase, induce, inhibit, mediate, mutate, prevent, promote, reduce, regulate, repress, signal, stimulate, suppress, transform, trigger

Table 1. Selected biomedical verbs and their types

2.2 Framesets of Biomedical Verbs

Annotation of BioProp is mainly based on Levin's verb classes, as defined in the VerbNet lexicon (Kipper et al., 2000). In VerbNet, the arguments of each verb are represented at the semantic level, and thus have associated semantic roles. However, since some verbs may have different usages in biomedical and newswire texts, it is necessary to customize the framesets of biomedical verbs. The 30 verbs in Table 1 are categorized into four types according to the degree of difference in usage: (1) verbs that do not appear in VerbNet due to their low frequency in the newswire domain; (2) verbs that do appear in VerbNet, but whose biomedical meanings and framesets are undefined; (3) verbs that do appear in VerbNet, but whose primary newswire and biomedical usage differ; (4) verbs that have the same usage in both domains.

Verbs of the first type play important roles in biomedical texts, but rarely appear in newswire texts and thus are not defined in VerbNet. For example, "phosphorylate" increasingly appears in the fast-growing PubMed abstracts that report experimental results on phosphorylated events; therefore, it is included in our verb list. However, since VerbNet does not define the frameset for "phosphorylate", we must define it after analyzing all the sentences in our corpus that contain the verb. Other type 1 verbs may correspond to verbs in VerbNet; in such cases, we can borrow the VerbNet definitions and framesets. For example, "transactivate" is not found in VerbNet, but we can adopt the frameset of "activate" for this verb.

Verbs of the second type appear in VerbNet, but have unique biomedical meanings that are undefined. Therefore, the framesets corresponding to their biomedical meanings must be added. In most cases, we can adopt framesets from VerbNet synonyms. For example, "express" is defined as "say" and "send very quickly" in VerbNet. However, in the biomedical domain, its usage is very similar to "translate". Thus, we can use the frameset of "translate" for "express". Table 2 shows the framesets and corresponding examples of "express" in the newswire domain and biomedical domain, as well as that of "translate" in VerbNet.

Verbs of the third type also appear in VerbNet. Although the newswire and biological senses are defined therein, their primary newswire sense is not the same as their primary biomedical sense. "Bind," for example, is common in the newswire domain, and it usually means "to tie" or "restrain with bonds." However, in the biomedical domain, its intransitive use- "attach or stick to"- is far more common. For example, a Google search for the phrase "glue binds to" only returned 21 results, while the same search replacing "glue" with "protein" yields 197,000 hits. For such verbs, we only need select the appropriate alternative meanings and corresponding framesets. Lastly, for verbs of the fourth type, we can directly adopt the newswire definitions and framesets, since they are identical.

2.3 Distribution of Selected Verbs

There is a significant difference between the occurrence of the 30 selected verbs in biomedical texts and their occurrence in newswire texts. The verbs appearing in verb phrases constitute only 1,297 PAS's, i.e., 1% of all PAS's, in PropBank (shown in Figure 2), compared to 2,382 PAS's, i.e., 16% of all PAS's, in BioProp (shown in Figure 3). Furthermore, some biomedical verbs have very few PAS's in PropBank, as shown in Table 3. The above observations indicate that it is necessary to annotate a biomedical proposition bank for training a biomedical SRL system.

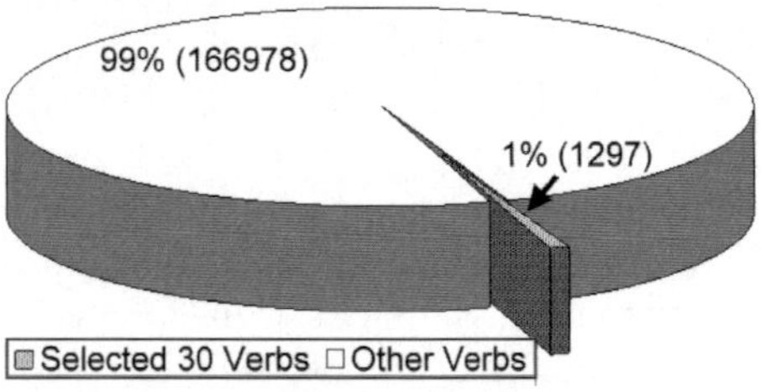

Figure 2. The percentage of the 30 biomedical verbs and other verbs in PropBank

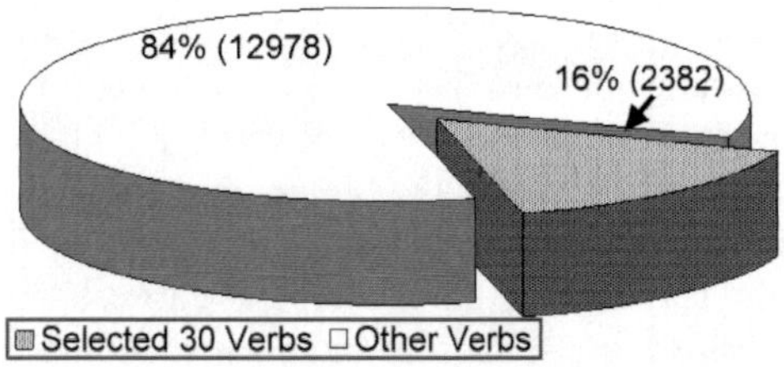

Figure 3. The percentage of the 30 biomedical verbs and other verbs in BioProp

Verbs	# in BioProp	Ratio(%)	# in PropBank	Ratio(%)
induce	290	1.89	16	0.01
bind	252	1.64	0	0
activate	235	1.53	2	0
express	194	1.26	53	0.03
inhibit	184	1.20	6	0
increase	166	1.08	396	0.24
regulate	122	0.79	23	0.01
mediate	104	0.68	1	0
stimulate	93	0.61	11	0.01
associate	82	0.53	51	0.03
encode	79	0.51	0	0
affect	60	0.39	119	0.07
enhance	60	0.39	28	0.02
block	58	0.38	71	0.04
reduce	55	0.36	241	0.14
decrease	54	0.35	16	0.01
suppress	38	0.25	4	0
interact	36	0.23	0	0
alter	27	0.18	17	0.01
transactivate	24	0.16	0	0
modulate	22	0.14	1	0
phosphorylate	21	0.14	0	0
transform	21	0.14	22	0.01
differentiate	21	0.14	2	0
repress	17	0.11	1	0
prevent	15	0.10	92	0.05
promote	14	0.09	52	0.03
trigger	14	0.09	40	0.02
mutate	14	0.09	1	0
signal	10	0.07	31	0.02

Table 3. The number and percentage of PAS's for each verb in BioProp and PropBank

3 Annotation of BioProp

3.1 Annotation Process

After choosing 30 verbs as predicates, we adopted a semi-automatic method to annotate BioProp. The annotation process consists of the following steps: (1) identifying predicate candidates; (2) automatically annotating the biomedical semantic roles with our WSJ SRL system; (3) transforming the automatic tagging results into *WordFreak* (Morton and LaCivita, 2003) format; and (4) manually correcting the annotation results with the *WordFreak* annotation tool. We now describe these steps in detail:

1. Each word with a VB POS tag in a verb phrase that matches any lexical variant of the 30 verbs is treated as a predicate candidate. The automatically selected targets are then double-checked by human annotators. As a result, 2,382 predicates were identified in BioProp.

2. Sentences containing the above 2,382 predicates were extracted and labeled automatically by our WSJ SRL system. In total, 7,764 arguments were identified.

3. In this step, sentences with PAS annotations are transformed into *WordFreak* format (an XML format), which allows annotators to view a sentence in a tree-like fashion. In addition, users can customize the tag set of arguments. Other linguistic information can also be integrated and displayed in

WordFreak, which is a convenient annotation tool.

4. In the last step, annotators check the predicted semantic roles using *WordFreak* and then correct or add semantic roles if the predicted arguments are incorrect or missing, respectively. Three biologists with sufficient biological knowledge in our laboratory performed the annotation task after receiving computational linguistic training for approximately three months.

Figure 4 illustrates an example of BioProp annotation displayed in *WordFreak* format, using the frameset of "phophorylate" listed in Table 4.

This annotation process can be used to construct a domain-specific corpus when a general-purpose tagging system is available. In our experience, this semi-automatic annotation scheme saves annotation efforts and improves the annotation consistency.

Predicate	Frameset
phosphorylate	**Arg0:** causer of phosphorylation **Arg1:** thing being phosphorylated **Arg2:** end state **Arg3:** start state

Table 4. The frameset of "phosphorylate"

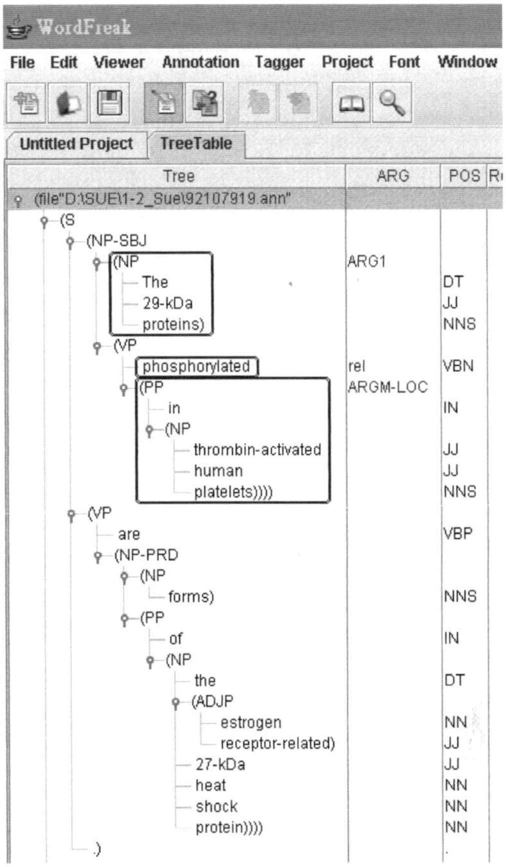

Figure 4. An example of BioProp displayed with *WordFreak*

3.2 Inter-annotation Agreement

We conducted preliminary consistency tests on 2,382 instances of biomedical propositions. The inter-annotation agreement was measured by the kappa statistic (Siegel and Castellan, 1988), the definition of which is based on the probability of inter-annotation agreement, denoted by $P(A)$, and the agreement expected by chance, denoted by $P(E)$. The kappa statistics for inter-annotation agreement were .94 for semantic role identification and .95 for semantic role classification when ArgM labels were included for evaluation. When ArgM labels were omitted, kappa statistics were .94 and .98 for identification and classification, respectively. We also calculated the results of combined decisions, i.e., identification and classification. (See Table 5.)

		$P(A)$	$P(E)$	Kappa score
including ArgM	role identification	.97	.52	.94
	role classification	.96	.18	.95
	combined decision	.96	.18	.95
excluding ArgM	role identification	.97	.26	.94
	role classification	.99	.28	.98
	combined decision	.99	.28	.98

Table 5. Inter-annotator agreement

3.3 Annotation Efforts

Since we employ a WSJ SRL system that labels semantic roles automatically, human annotators can quickly browse and determine correct tagging results; thus, they do not have to examine all tags during the annotation process, as in the full manual annotation approach. Only incorrectly predicted tags need to be modified, and missed tags need to be added. Therefore, annotation efforts can be substantially reduced. To quantify the reduction in annotation efforts, we define the saving of annotation effort, ρ, as:

$$\rho = \frac{\#\text{of correctly labeled nodes}}{\#\text{of all nodes}} < \frac{\#\text{of correctly labeled nodes}}{\#\text{of correct} + \#\text{of incorrect} + \#\text{of missed nodes}} \quad (1)$$

In Equation (1), since the number of nodes that need to be examined is usually unknown, we use an easy approximation to obtain an upper bound for ρ. This is based on the extremely optimistic assumption that annotators should be able to recover a missed or incorrect label by only checking one node. However, in reality, this would be impossible. In our annotation process, the upper bound of ρ for BioProp is given by:

$$\rho < \frac{18932}{18932+6682+15316} = \frac{18932}{40975} = 46\%,$$

which means that, at most, the annotation effort could be reduced by 46%.

A more accurate tagging system is preferred because the more accurate the tagging system, the higher the upper bound ρ will be.

4 Disambiguation of Argument Annotation

During the annotation process, we encountered a number of problems resulting from different usage of vocabulary and writing styles in general English and the biomedical domain. In this section, we describe three major problems and propose our solutions.

4.1 Cue Words for Role Classification

PropBank annotation guidelines provide a list of words that can help annotators decide an argument's type. Similarly, we add some rules to our BioProp annotation guideline. For example, "in vivo" and "in vitro" are used frequently in biomedical literature; however, they seldom appear in general English articles. According to their meanings, we classify them as location argument (AM-LOC).

In addition, some words occur frequently in both general English and in biomedical domains but have different meanings/usages. For instance, "development" is often tagged as Arg0 or Arg1 in general English, as shown by the following sentence:

Despite the strong case for stocks, however, most pros warn that [individuals$_{\text{Arg0}}$] shouldn't try to [profit$_{\text{predicate}}$] [from short-term developments$_{\text{Arg1}}$].

However, in the biomedical domain, "development" always means the stage of a disease, cell, etc. Therefore, we tag it as temporal argument (AM-TMP), as shown in the following sentence:

[Rhom-2 mRNA$_{\text{Arg1}}$] is [expressed$_{\text{predicate}}$] [in early mouse development$_{\text{AM-TMP}}$] [in central nervous system, lung, kidney, liver, and spleen but only very low levels occur in thymus$_{\text{AM-LOC}}$].

4.2 Additional Argument Types

In PropBank, the negative argument (AM-NEG) usually contains explicit negative words such as "not". However, in the biomedical domain, researchers usually express negative meaning implicitly by using "fail", "unable", "inability", "neither", "nor", "failure", etc. Take "fail" as an example. It is tagged as a verb in general English, as shown in the following sentence:

But [the new pact$_{\text{Arg1}}$] will force huge debt on the new firm and [could$_{\text{AM-MOD}}$] [still$_{\text{AM-TMP}}$] [fail$_{\text{predicate}}$] [to thwart rival suitor McCaw Cellular$_{\text{Arg2}}$].

Negative results are important in the biomedical domain. Thus, for annotation purposes, we create additional negation tag (AM-NEG1) that does not exist in PropBank. The following sentence is an example showing the use of AM-NEG1:

[They$_{\text{Arg0}}$] [fail$_{\text{AM-NEG1}}$] to [induce$_{\text{predicate}}$] [mRNA of TNF-alpha$_{\text{Arg1}}$] [after 3 h of culture $_{\text{AM-TMP}}$].

In this example, if we do not introduce the AM-NEG1, "fail" is considered as a verb like in PropBank, not as a negative argument, and it will not be included in the proposition for the predicate "induce". Thus, BioProp requires the "AM-NEG1" tag to precisely express the corresponding proposition.

4.3 Essentiality of Biomedical Knowledge

Since PAS's contain more semantic information, proposition bank annotators require more domain knowledge than annotators of other corpora. In BioProp, many ambiguous expressions require biomedical knowledge to correctly annotate them, as exemplified by the following sentence in BioProp:

In the cell types tested, the LS mutations indicated an apparent requirement not only for the intact NF-kappa B and SP1-binding sites but also for [several regions between -201 and -130$_{\text{Arg1}}$] [not$_{\text{AM-NEG}}$] [previously$_{\text{AM-MNR}}$] [associated$_{\text{predicate}}$][with viral infectivity$_{\text{Arg2}}$].

Annotators without biomedical knowledge may consider [between -201 and -130] as extent argument (AM-EXT), because the PropBank guidelines define numerical adjuncts as AM-

EXT. However, it means a segment of DNA. It is an appositive of [several regions]; therefore, it should be annotated as part of Arg1 in this case.

5 Effect of Training Corpora on SRL Systems

To examine the possibility that BioProp can improve the training of SRL systems used for automatic tagging of biomedical texts, we compare the performance of systems trained on BioProp and PropBank in different domains. We construct a new SRL system (called a BIOmedical SeMantIc roLe labEler, BIOSMILE) that is trained on BioProp and employs all the features used in our WSJ SRL system (Tsai et al., 2006).

As with POS tagging, chunking, and named entity recognition, SRL can also be formulated as a sentence tagging problem. A sentence can be represented by a sequence of words, a sequence of phrases, or a parsing tree; the basic units of a sentence in these representations are words, phrases, and constituents, respectively. Hacioglu et al. (2004) showed that tagging phrase-by-phrase (P-by-P) is better than word-by-word (W-by-W). However, Punyakanok et al. (2004) showed that constituent-by-constituent (C-by-C) tagging is better than P-by-P. Therefore, we use C-by-C tagging for SRL in our BIOSMILE.

SRL can be divided into two steps. First, we identify all the predicates. This can be easily accomplished by finding all instances of verbs of interest and checking their part-of-speech (POS) tags. Second, we label all arguments corresponding to each predicate. This is a difficult problem, since the number of arguments and their positions vary according to a verb's voice (active/passive) and sense, along with many other factors.

In BIOSMILE, we employ the maximum entropy (ME) model for argument classification. We use Zhang's MaxEnt toolkit (http://www.nlplab.cn/zhangle/maxent_toolkit.html) and the L-BFGS (Nocedal and Wright, 1999) method of parameter estimation for our ME model. Table 6 shows the features we employ in BIOSMILE and our WSJ SRL system.

To compare the effects of using biomedical training data versus using general English data, we train BIOSMILE on 30 randomly selected training sets from BioProp (g_1,.., g_{30}), and WSJ SRL system on 30 from PropBank (w_1,.., w_{30}), each of which has 1,200 training PAS's.

BASIC FEATURES

- **Predicate** – The predicate lemma
- **Path** – The syntactic path through the parsing tree from the parse constituent being classified to the predicate
- **Constituent type**
- **Position** – Whether the phrase is located before or after the predicate
- **Voice** – passive: If the predicate has a POS tag VBN, and its chunk is not a VP, or it is preceded by a form of "to be" or "to get" within its chunk; otherwise, it is active
- **Head word** – Calculated using the head word table described by Collins (1999)
- **Head POS** – The POS of the Head Word
- **Sub-categorization** – The phrase structure rule that expands the predicate's parent node in the parsing tree
- **First and last Word and their POS tags**
- **Level** – The level in the parsing tree

PREDICATE FEATURES

- **Predicate's verb class**
- **Predicate POS tag**
- **Predicate frequency**
- **Predicate's context POS**
- **Number of predicates**

FULL PARSING FEATURES

- **Parent's, left sibling's, and right sibling's paths, constituent types, positions, head words and head POS tags**
- **Head of PP parent** – If the parent is a PP, then the head of this PP is also used as a feature

COMBINATION FEATURES

- **Predicate distance combination**
- **Predicate phrase type combination**
- **Head word and predicate combination**
- **Voice position combination**

OTHERS

- **Syntactic frame of predicate/NP**
- **Headword suffixes of lengths 2, 3, and 4**
- **Number of words in the phrase**
- **Context words & POS tags**

Table 6. The features used in our argument classification model

We then test both systems on 30 400-PAS test sets from BioProp, with g_1 and w_1 being tested on test set 1, g_2 and w_2 on set 2, and so on. Then we generate the scores for g_1-g_{30} and w_1-w_{30}, and compare their averages.

Table 7 shows the experimental results. When tested on the biomedical corpus, BIOSMILE outperforms the WSJ SRL system by 22.9%. This result is statistically significant as expected.

Training	Test	Precision	Recall	F-score
PropBank	BioProp	74.78	56.25	64.20
BioProp	BioProp	88.65	85.61	87.10

Table 7. Performance comparison of SRL systems trained on BioProp and PropBank

6 Conclusion & Future Work

The primary contribution of this study is the annotation of a biomedical proposition bank that incorporates the following features. First, the choice of 30 representative biomedical verbs is made according to their frequency and importance in the biomedical domain. Second, since some of the verbs have different usages and others do not appear in the WSJ proposition bank, we redefine their framesets and add some new argument types. Third, the annotation guidelines in PropBank are slightly modified to suit the needs of the biomedical domain. Fourth, using appropriate argument types, framesets and annotation guidelines, we construct a biomedical proposition bank, BioProp, on top of the popular biomedical GENIA Treebank. Finally, we employ a semi-automatic annotation approach that uses an SRL system trained on the WSJ PropBank. Incorrect tagging results are then corrected by human annotators. This approach reduces annotation efforts significantly. For example, in BioProp, the annotation efforts can be reduced by, at most, 46%. In addition, trained on BioProp, BIOSMILE's F-score increases by 22.9% compared to the SRL system trained on the PropBank.

In our future work, we will investigate more biomedical verbs. Besides, since there are few biomedical treebanks, we plan to integrate full parsers in order to annotate syntactic and semantic information simultaneously. It will then be possible to apply the SRL techniques more extensively to biomedical relation extraction.

References

Ann Bies, Mark Ferguson, Karen Katz, and Robert MacIntyre. 1995. Bracketing Guidelines for Treebank II Style Penn Treebank Project. *Technical report, University of Pennsylvania.*

Xavier Carreras and Lluís Màrquez. 2005. Introduction to the CoNLL-2005 Shared Task: Semantic Role Labeling. *In Proceedings of CoNLL-2005.*

Michael Collins. 1999. Head-driven Statistical Models for Natural Language Parsing. Ph.D. thesis, University of Pennsylvania.

Kadri Hacioglu, Sameer Pradhan, Wayne Ward, James H. Martin, and Daniel Jurafsky. 2004. Semantic Role Labeling by Tagging Syntactic Chunks. *In Proceedings of CoNLL-2004.*

Jin-Dong Kim, Tomoko Ohta, Yuka Teteisi, and Jun'-ichi Tsujii. 2003. GENIA corpus—a semantically annotated corpus for bio-textmining. *Bioinformatics*, 19(Suppl. 1): i180-i182.

Karin Kipper, Hoa Trang Dang, and Martha Palmer. 2000. Class-based construction of a verb lexicon. *In Proceedings of AAAI-2000.*

Karin Kipper, Martha Palmer, and Owen Rambow. 2002. Extending PropBank with VerbNet semantic predicates. *In Proceedings of AMTA-2002.*

Mitchell Marcus, Grace Kim, Mary Ann Marcinkiewicz, Robert MacIntyre, Ann Bies, Mark Ferguson, Karen Katz, and Britta Schasberger. 1994. The Penn Treebank: Annotating predicate argument structure. *In Proceedings of ARPA Human Language Technology Workshop.*

Mitchell P. Marcus, Beatrice Santorini, and Mary Ann Marcinkiewicz. 1993. Building a large annotated corpus of English: the Penn Treebank. *Computational Linguistics*, 19(2): 313-330.

Thomas Morton and Jeremy LaCivita. 2003. WordFreak: an open tool for linguistic annotation. *In Proceedings of HLT/NAACL-2003.*

Jorge Nocedal and Stephen J Wright. 1999. *Numerical Optimization*, Springer.

Martha Palmer, Daniel Gildea, and Paul Kingsbury. 2005. The Proposition Bank: An Annotated Corpus of Semantic Roles. *Computational Linguistics*, 31(1).

Vasin Punyakanok, Dan Roth, Wen-tau Yih, and Dav Zimak. 2004. Semantic Role Labeling via Integer Linear Programming Inference. *In Proceedings of COLING-2004.*

Sidney Siegel and N. John Castellan. 1988. *Nonparametric Statistics for the Behavioral Sciences.* New York, McGraw-Hill.

Richard Tzong-Han Tsai, Wen-Chi Chou, Yu-Chun Lin, Cheng-Lung Sung, Wei Ku, Ying-Shan Su, Ting-Yi Sung, and Wen-Lian Hsu. 2006. BIOSMILE: Adapting Semantic Role Labeling for Biomedical Verbs: An Exponential Model Coupled with Automatically Generated Template Features. *In Proceedings of BioNLP'06.*

Yuka Tateisi, Tomoko Ohta, and Jun-ichi Tsujii. 2004. Annotation of Predicate-argument Structure of Molecular Biology Text. *In Proceedings of the IJCNLP-04 workshop on Beyond Shallow Analyses.*

Yuka Tateisi and Jun-ichi Tsujii. 2004. Part-of-Speech Annotation of Biology Research Abstracts. *In Proceedings of the 4th International Conference on Language Resource and Evaluation.*

Yuka Tateisi, Akane Yakushiji, Tomoko Ohta, and Jun-ichi Tsujii. 2005. Syntax Annotation for the GENIA corpus. *In Proceedings of IJCNLP-2005.*

Tuangthong Wattarujeekrit, Parantu K Shah, and Nigel Collier1. 2004. PASBio: predicate-argument structures for event extraction in molecular biology. *BMC Bioinformatics*, 5(155).

Nianwen Xue and Martha Palmer. 2004. Calibrating Features for Semantic Role Labeling. *In Proceedings of the EMNLP-2004.*

Xiaofeng Yang, Guodong Zhou, Jian Su, and Chew Lim Tan. 2004. Improving Noun Phrase Coreference Resolution by Matching Strings. *In Proceedings of 1st International Joint Conference on Natural Language Processing*: 226-233.

How and Where do People Fail with Time: Temporal Reference Mapping Annotation by Chinese and English Bilinguals

Yang Ye[§]**, Steven Abney**[†§]
[†]Department of Linguistics
[§]Department of Electrical Engineering and Computer Science
University of Michigan

Abstract

This work reports on three human tense annotation experiments for Chinese verbs in Chinese-to-English translation scenarios. The results show that inter-annotator agreement increases as the context of the verb under the annotation becomes increasingly specified, i.e. as the context moves from the situation in which the target English sentence is unknown to the situation in which the target lexicon and target syntactic structure are fully specified. The annotation scheme with a fully specified syntax and lexicon in the target English sentence yields a satisfactorily high agreement rate. The annotation results were then analyzed via an ANOVA analysis, a logistic regression model and a log-linear model. The analyses reveal that while both the overt and the latent linguistic factors seem to significantly affect annotation agreement under different scenarios, the latent features are the real driving factors of tense annotation disagreement among multiple annotators. The analyses also find the verb telicity feature, aspect marker presence and syntactic embedding structure to be strongly associated with tense, suggesting their utility in the automatic tense classification task.

1 Introduction

In recent years, the research community has seen a fast-growing volume of work in temporal information processing. Consequently, the investigation and practice of temporal information annotation by human experts have emerged from the corpus annotation research. To evaluate automatic temporal relation classification systems, annotated corpora must be created and validated, which motivates experiments and research in temporal information annotation.

One important temporal relation distinction that human beings make is the temporal reference distinction based on relative positioning between the following three time parameters, as proposed by (Reichenbach, 1947): speech time (S), event time (E) and reference time (R). Temporal reference distinction is linguistically realized as tenses. Languages have various granularities of tense representations; some have finer-grained tenses or aspects than others. This poses a great challenge to automatic cross-lingual tense mapping. The same challenge holds for cross-lingual tense annotation, especially for language pairs that have dramatically different tense strategies. A decent solution for cross-lingual tense mapping will benefit a variety of NLP tasks such as Machine Translation, Cross-lingual Question Answering (CLQA), and Multi-lingual Information Summarization. While automatic cross-lingual tense mapping has recently started to receive research attention, such as in (Olsen,et al., 2001) and (Ye, et al., 2005), to the best of our knowledge, human performance on tense and aspect annotation for machine translation between English and Chinese has not received any systematic investigation to date. Cross-linguistic NLP tasks, especially those requiring a more accurate tense and aspect resolution, await a more focused study of human tense and aspect annotation performance.

Chinese and English are a language pair in which tense and aspect are represented at different levels of units: one being realized at the word level and the other at the morpheme level.

This paper reports on a series of cross-linguistic tense annotation experiments between Chinese and English, and provides statistical inference for different linguistic factors via a series of statistical modeling. Since tense and aspect are morphologically merged in English, tense annotation

Proceedings of the Workshop on Frontiers in Linguistically Annotated Corpora 2006, pages 13–20,
Sydney, July 2006.

discussed in this paper also includes elements of aspect. We only deal with tense annotation in Chinese-to-English scenario in the scope of this paper.

The remaining part of the paper is organized as follows: Section 2 summarizes the significant related works in temporal information annotation and points out how this study relates to yet differs from them. Section 3 reports the details of three tense annotation experiments under three scenarios. Section 4 discusses the inter-judge agreement by presenting two measures of agreement: the Kappa Statistic and accuracy-based measurement. Section 5 investigates and reports on the significance of different linguistic factors in tense annotation via an ANOVA analysis, a logistic regression analysis and a log-linear model analysis. Finally, section 6 concludes the paper and points out directions for future research.

2 Related Work

There are two basic types of temporal location relationships. The first one is the ternary classification of past, present and future. The second one is the binary classification of "BEFORE" versus "AFTER". These two types of temporal relationships are intrinsically related but each stands as a separate issue and is dealt with in different works. While the "BEFORE" versus "AFTER" relationship can easily be transferred across a language pair, the ternary tense taxonomy is often very hard to transfer from one language to another.

(Wilson, et al., 1997) describes a multilingual approach to annotating temporal information, which involves flagging a temporal expression in the document and identifying the time value that the expression designates. Their work reports an inter-annotator reliability F-measure of 0.79 and 0.86 respectively for English corpora.

(Katz, et al., 2001) describes a simple and general technique for the annotation of temporal relation information based on binary interval relation types: precedence and inclusion. Their annotation scheme could benefit a range of NLP applications and is easy to carry out.

(Pustejovsky et al., 2004) reports an annotation scheme, the TimeML metadata, for the markup of events and their anchoring in documents. The annotation schema of TimeML is very fine-grained with a wide coverage of different event types, dependencies between events and times, as well as "LINK" tags which encode the various relations existing between the temporal elements of a document. The challenge of human labeling of links among eventualities was discussed at great length in their paper. Automatic "time-stamping" was attempted on a small sample of text in an earlier work of (Mani, 2003). The result was not particularly promising. It showed the need for a larger quantity of training data as well as more predictive features, especially on the discourse level. At the word level, the semantic representation of tenses could be approached in various ways depending on different applications. So far, their work has gone the furthest towards establishing a broad and open standard metadata mark-up language for natural language texts.

(Setzer, et al., 2004) presents a method of evaluating temporal order relation annotations and an approach to facilitate the creation of a gold standard by introducing the notion of temporal closure, which can be deduced from any annotations through using a set of inference rules.

From the above works, it can be seen that the effort in temporal information annotation has thus far been dominated by annotating temporal relations that hold entities such as events or times explicitly mentioned in the text. Cross-linguistic tense and aspect annotation has so far gone unstudied.

3 Chinese Tense Annotation Experiments[1]

In current section, we present three tense annotation experiments with the following scenarios:

1. Null-control situation by native Chinese speakers where the annotators were provided with the source Chinese sentences but not the English translations;

2. High-control situation by native English speakers where the annotators were provided with the Chinese sentences as well as English translations with specified syntax and lexicons;

3. Semi-control situation by native English speakers where the annotators were allowed to choose the syntax and lexicons for the English sentence with appropriate tenses;

[1] All experiments in the paper are approved by Behavioral Sciences Institutional Review Board at the University of Michigan, the IRB file number is B04-00007481-I.

3.1 Experiment One

Experiment One presents the first scenario of tense annotation for Chinese verbs in Chinese-to-English cross-lingual situation. In the first scenario, the annotation experiment was carried out on 25 news articles from LDC Xinhua News release with category number LDC2001T11. The articles were divided into 5 groups with 5 articles in each group. There are a total number of 985 verbs. For each group, three native Chinese speakers who were bilingual in Chinese and English annotated the tense of the verbs in the articles independently. Prior to annotating the data, the annotators underwent brief training during which they were asked to read an example of a Chinese sentence for each tense and make sure they understand the examples. During the annotation, the annotators were asked to read the whole articles first and then select a tense tag based on the context of each verb. The tense taxonomy provided to the annotators include the twelve tenses that are different combinations of the simple tenses (present, past and future), the prograssive aspect and the perfect aspect. In cases where the judges were unable to decide the tense of a verb, they were instructed to tag it as "unknown". In this experiment, the annotators were asked to tag the tense for all Chinese words that were tagged as verbs in the Penn Treebank corpora. Conceivably, the task under the current scenario is meta-linguistic in nature for the reason that tense is an elusive notion for Chinese speakers. Nevertheless, the experiment provides a baseline situation for human tense annotation agreement. The following is an example of the annotation where the annotators were to choose an appropriate tense tag from the provided tense tags:

((IP (NP-TPC (NP-PN (NR 中国))(NP (NN 建筑)(NN 市场)))(LCP-TMP (NP (NT 近年))(LC 来)) (NP-SBJ (NP (PP (P 对)(NP (NN 外)))(NP (NN 开放)))(NP (NN 步伐)))(VP (ADVP (AD 进一步)) (VP (***VV 加快***)))(PU 。)))

1. simple present tense
2. simple past tense
3. simple future tense
4. present perfect tense
5. past perfect tense
6. future perfect tense
7. present progressive tense
8. past progressive tense
9. future progressive
10. present perfect progressive
11. past perfect progressive

3.2 Experiment Two

Experiment Two was carried out using 25 news articles from the parallel Chinese and English news articles available from LDC Multiple Translation Chinese corpora (MTC catalog number LDC2002T01). In the previous experiment, the annotators tagged all verbs. In the current experimental set-up, we preprocessed the materials and removed those verbs that lose their verbal status in translation from Chinese to English due to nominalization. After this preprocessing, there was a total of 288 verbs annotated by the annotators. Three native speakers, who were bilingually fluent in English and Chinese, were recruited to annotate the tense for the English verbs that were translated from Chinese. As in the previous scenario, the annotators were encouraged to pay attention to the context of the target verb when tagging its tense. The annotators were provided with the full taxonomy illustrated by examples of English verbs and they worked independently. The following is an example of the annotation where the annotators were to choose an appropriate tense tag from the provided tense tags:

据统计，这些城市去年***完成***国内生产总值一百九十多亿元，比开放前的一九九一年增长九成多。
According to statistics, the cities (***achieve***) a combined gross domestic product of RMB19 billion last year, an increase of more than 90% over 1991 before their opening.

A. achieves
B. achieved
C. will achieve
D. are achieving
E. were achieving
F. will be achieving
G. have achieved
H. had achieved
I. will have achieved
J. have been achieving
K. had been achieving
L. will have been achieving
M. would achieve

3.3 Experiment Three

Experiment Three was an experiment simulated on 52 Xinhua news articles from the Multiple Translation Corpus (MTC) mentioned in the previous section. Since in the MTC corpora, each Chinese article is translated into English by ten human translation teams, conceptually, we could view these ten translation teams as different annotators. They were making decisions about appropriate tense for the English verbs. These annotators differ from those in Experiment Two described above in that they were allowed to choose any syntactic structure and verb lexicon. This is because they were performing tense annotation in a bigger task of sentence translation. Therefore, their tense annotations were performed with much less specification of the annotation context. We manually aligned the Chinese verbs with the English verbs for the 10 translation teams from the MTC corpora and thus obtained our third source of tense annotation results. For the Chinese verbs that were not translated as verbs into English, we assigned a "Not Available" tag. There are 1505 verbs in total including the ones that lost their verbal status across the language.

4 Inter-Judge Agreement

Researchers use consistency checking to validate human annotation experiments. There are various ways of performing consistency checking described in the literature, depending on the scale of the measurements. Each has its advantages and disadvantages. Since our tense taxonomy is nominal without any ordinal information, Kappa statistics measurement is the most appropriate choice to measure inter-judge agreement.

4.1 Kappa Statistic

Kappa scores were calculated for the three human judges' annotation results. The Kappa score is the de facto standard for evaluating inter-judge agreement on tagging tasks. It reports the agreement rate among multiple annotators while correcting for the agreement brought about by pure chance. It is defined by the following formula, where P(A) is the observed agreement among the judges and P(E) is the expected agreement:

$$k = \frac{P(A) - P(E)}{1 - P(E)} \quad (1)$$

Depending on how one identifies the expected agreement brought about by pure chance, there are two ways to calculate the Kappa score. One is the "Seigel-Castellian" Kappa discussed in (Eugenio, 2004), which assumes that there is one hypothetical distribution of labels for all judges. In contrast, the "Cohen" Kappa discussed in (Cohen, 1960), assumes that each annotator has an individual distribution of labels. This discrepancy slightly affects the calculation of P(E). There is no consensus regarding which Kappa is the "right" one and researchers use both. In our experiments, we use the "Seigel-Castellian" Kappa.

The Kappa statistic for the annotation results of Experiment One are 0.277 on the full taxonomy and 0.37 if we collapse the tenses into three big classes: present, past and future. The observed agreement rate,that is, P(A), is 0.42.

The Kappa score for tense resolution from the ten human translation teams for the 52 Xinhua news articles is 0.585 on the full taxonomy; we expect the Kappa score to be higher if we exclude the verbs that are nominalized. Interestingly, the Kappa score calculated by collapsing the 13 tenses into 3 tenses (present, past and future) is only slightly higher: 0.595. The observed agreement rate is 0.72.

Human tense annotation in the Chinese-to-English restricted translation scenario achieved a Kappa score of 0.723 on the full taxonomy with an observed agreement of 0.798. If we collapse simple past and present perfect, the Kappa score goes up to 0.792 with an observed agreement of 0.893. The Kappa score is 0.81 on the reduced taxonomy.

4.2 Accuracy

The Kappa score is a relatively conservative measurement of the inter-judge agreement rate. Conceptually, we could also obtain an alternative measurement of reliability by taking one annotator as the gold standard at one time and averaging over the accuracies of the different annotators across different gold standards. While it is true that numerically, this would yield a higher score than the Kappa score and seems to be inflating the agreement rate, we argue that the difference between the Kappa score and the accuracy-based measurement is not limited to one being more aggressive than the other. The policies of these two measurements are different. The Kappa score is concerned purely with agreement without any consideration of truthfulness or falsehood, while the procedure we described above gives equal weights to each annotator being the gold standard. Therefore, it considers both the agreement and the truthfulness of the annotation. Additionally, the accuracy-based measurement is the same measurement that is typically used to evaluate machine performance; therefore it gives a genuine ceiling for machine performance.

The accuracy under such a scheme for the three annotators in Experiment One is 43% on the full tense taxonomy.

The accuracy under such a scheme for tense generation agreement from three annotators in Experiment Two is 80% on the full tense taxonomy.

The accuracy under such a scheme for the ten translation teams in Experiment Three is 70.8% on the full tense taxonomy.

Table 1 summarizes the inter-judge agreement for the three experiments.

Examining the annotation results, we identified the following sources of disagreement. While the

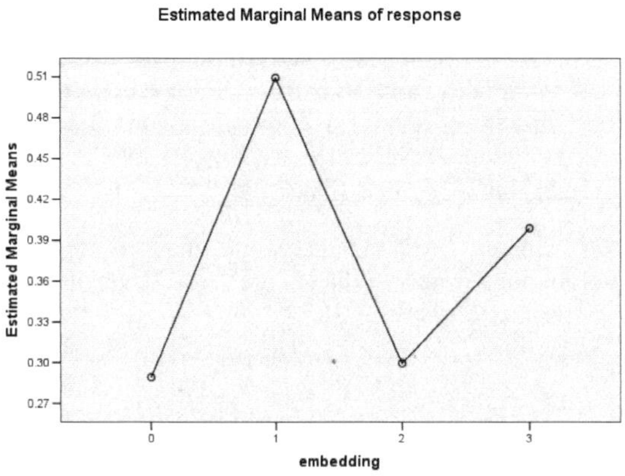

Figure 3: Effect of Syntactic Embedding Structure on Tense Annotation Disagreement

pect this is partly due to the correlation between the punctuality feature and the telicity feature. Additionally, none of the overt linguistic features is significant in the presence of the latent features, which implies that the latent features drive disagreement among multiple annotators.

5.3 Log-linear Model Analysis of Associations between Linguistic Factors in Free Translation Tense Annotation

This section discusses the association patterns between tense and the relevant linguistic factors via a log-linear model. A log-linear model is a special case of generalized linear models (GLMs) and has been widely applied in many fields of social science research for multivariate analysis of categorical data. The model reveals the interaction between categorical variables. The log-linear model is different from other GLMs in that it does not distinguish between "response" and "explanatory variables". All variables are treated alike as "response variables", whose mutual associations are explored. Under the log-linear model, the expected cell frequencies are functions of all variables in the model. The most parsimonious model that produces the smallest discrepancy between the expected cell and the observed cell frequencies is chosen as the final model. This provides the best explanation of the observed relationships among variables.

We use the data from Experiment Two for the current analysis. The results show that three linguistic features under investigation are significantly associated with tense. First, there is a strong association between aspect marker presence and tense, independent of punctuality, telicity feature and embedding structure. Second, there is a strong association between telicity and tense, independent of punctuality, aspect marker presence and punctuality feature. Thirdly, there is a strong association between embedding structure and tense, independent of telicity, punctuality feature and aspect marker presence. This result is consistent with (Olsen, 2001), in that the lexical telicity feature, when used heuristically as the single knowledge source, can achieve a good prediction of verb tense in Chinese to English Machine Translation. For example, the odds of the verb being atelic in the past tense is 2.5 times the odds of the verb being atelic in the future tense, with a 95% confidence interval of (0.9, 7.2). And the odds of a verb in the future tense having an aspect marker approaches zero when compared to the odds of a verb in the past tense having an aspect marker.

Putting together the pieces from the logistic analysis and the current analysis, we see that annotators fail to agree on tense selection mostly with apunctual verbs, while the agreed-upon tense is jointly decided by the telicity feature, aspect marker feature and the syntactic embedding structure that are associated with the verb.

6 Conclusions and Future Work

As the initial attempt to assess human beings' cross-lingual tense annotation, the current paper carries out a series of tense annotation experiments between Chinese and English under different scenarios. We show that even if tense is an abstract grammatical category, multiple annotators are still able to achieve a good agreement rate when the target English context is fully specified. We also show that in a non-restricted scenario, the overt linguistic features (aspect markers, embedding structures and temporal modifiers), can cause people to fail to agree with each other significantly in tense annotation. These factors exhibit certain interaction patterns in the decision making of the annotators. Our analysis of the annotation results from the scenario with a fully specified context show that people tend to fail to agree with each other on tense for verbs associated with interval events. The disagreement seems not to be driven by the overt linguistic features such as embedding structure and aspect markers. Lastly, among a set of overt and latent linguistic features, aspect marker presence, embedding structure and the telicity feature exhibit the strongest association with tense, potentially indicating their high utility in tense classification task.

The current analysis, while suggesting certain interesting patterns in tense annotation, could be more significant if the findings could be replicated by experiments of different scales on different data sets. Furthermore, the statistical analysis could be more finely geared to capture the more subtle distinctions encoded in the features.

Acknowledgement All of the annotation experiments in this paper are funded by Rackham Graduate School's Discretionary Funds at the University of Michigan.

References

Hans Reichenbach,1947. Elements of Symbolic Logic, Macmillan, New York, N.Y.

Mari Olson, David Traum, Carol Van Ess-Dykema, and Amy Weinberg, 2001. Implicit Cues for Explicit Generation: Using Telicity as a Cue for Tense Structure in a Chinese to English MT System, Proceedings Machine Translation Summit VIII, Santiago de Compostela, Spain.

Yang Ye, Zhu Zhang, 2005. Tense Tagging for Verbs in Cross-Lingual Context: A Case Study. Proceedings of 2nd International Joint Conference in Natural Language Processing (IJCNLP), 885-895.

George Wilson, Inderjeet Mani, Beth Sundheim, and Lisa Ferro, 2001. A Multilingual Approach to Annotating and Extracting Temporal Information, Proceedings of the ACL 2001 Workshop on Temporal And Spatial Information Processing, 39th Annual Meeting of ACL, Toulouse, 81-87.

Graham Katz and Fabrizio Arosio, 2001. The Annotation of Temporal Information in Natural Language Sentences, Proceedings of the ACL 2001 Workshop on Temporal And Spatial Information Processing, 39th Annual Meeting of ACL, Toulouse, 104-111.

James Pustejovsky, Robert Ingria, Roser Sauri, Jose Castano, Jessica Littman, Rob Gaizauskas, Andrea Setzer, Graham Katz, and Inderjeet Mani. 2004. The Specification Language TimeML. The Language of Time: A Reader. Oxford, 185-96.

Barbara Di Eugenio and Michael Glass. 2004. The kappa statistic: A second look. Computational Linguistics, 30(1): 95-101.

Inderjeet Mani, 2003. Recent Developments in Temporal Information Extraction. In Nicolov, N. and Mitkov, R., editors, Proceedings of RANLP'03. John Benjamins.

Andrea Setzer, Robert Gaizauskas, and Mark Hepple, 2003. Using Semantic Inferences for Temporal Annotation Comparison, Proceedings of the Fourth International Workshop on Inference in Computational Semantics (ICOS-4), INRIA, Lorraine, Nancy, France, September 25-26, 185-96.

Jacob Cohen, 1960. A Coefficient of Agreement for Nominal Scales, Educational and Psychological Measurement, 20, 37-46.

Probing the space of grammatical variation: induction of cross-lingual grammatical constraints from treebanks

Felice Dell'Orletta
Università di Pisa, Dipartimento di Informatica - Largo B. Pontecorvo 3
ILC-CNR - via G. Moruzzi 1
56100 Pisa, Italy
felice.dellorletta@ilc.cnr.it

Alessandro Lenci
Università di Pisa, Dipartimento di Linguistica - Via Santa Maria 36
56100 Pisa, Italy
alessandro.lenci@ilc.cnr.it

Simonetta Montemagni
ILC-CNR - via G. Moruzzi 1
56100 Pisa, Italy
simonetta.montemagni@ilc.cnr.it

Vito Pirrelli
ILC-CNR - via G. Moruzzi 1
56100 Pisa, Italy
vito.pirrelli@ilc.cnr.it

Abstract

The paper reports on a detailed quantitative analysis of distributional language data of both Italian and Czech, highlighting the relative contribution of a number of distributed grammatical factors to sentence-based identification of subjects and direct objects. The work uses a Maximum Entropy model of stochastic resolution of conflicting grammatical constraints and is demonstrably capable of putting explanatory theoretical accounts to the test of usage-based empirical verification.

1 Introduction

The paper illustrates the application of a *Maximum Entropy* (henceforth MaxEnt) model (Ratnaparkhi 1998) to the processing of subjects and direct objects in Italian and Czech. The model makes use of richly annotated Treebanks to determine the types of linguistic factors involved in the task and weigh up their relative salience. In doing so, we set ourselves a two-fold goal. On the one hand, we intend to discuss the use of Treebanks to discover typologically relevant and linguistically motivated factors and assess the relative contribution of the latter to cross-linguistic parsing issues. On the other hand, we are interested in testing the empirical plausibility of constraint-resolution models of language processing (see infra) when confronted with real language data.

Current research in natural language learning and processing supports the view that grammatical competence consists in mastering and integrating multiple, parallel constraints (Seidenberg and MacDonald 1999, MacWhinney 2004). Moreover, there is growing consensus on two major properties of grammatical constraints: i.) they are probabilistic "soft constraints" (Bresnan *et al.* 2001), and ii.) they have an inherently functional nature, involving different types of linguistic (and non linguistic) information (syntactic, semantic, etc.). These features emerge particularly clearly in dealing with one of the core aspects of grammar learning: the ability to identify *syntactic relations* in text. Psycholinguistic evidence shows that speakers learn to identify sentence subjects and direct objects by combining various types of probabilistic, functional cues, such as word order, noun animacy, definiteness, agreement, etc. An important observation is that the relative prominence of each such cue can considerably vary cross-linguistically. Bates *et al.* (1984), for example, argue that while, in English, word order is the most effective cue for Subject-Object Identification (henceforth *SOI*) both in syntactic processing and during the child's syntactic development, the same cue plays second fiddle in relatively free phrase-order languages such as Italian or German.

If grammatical constraints are inherently probabilistic (Manning 2003), the path through which adult grammar competence is acquired can be viewed as the process of building a stochastic model out of the linguistic input. In computational linguistics, MaxEnt models have

Proceedings of the Workshop on Frontiers in Linguistically Annotated Corpora 2006, pages 21–28,
Sydney, July 2006.

proven to be robust statistical learning algorithms that perform well in a number of processing tasks. Being supervised learning models, they require richly annotated data as training input. Before we turn to the use of Treebanks for training a MaxEnt model for *SOI*, we first analyse the range of linguistic factors that are taken to play a significant role in the task.

2 Subjects and objects in Czech and Italian

Grammatical relations - such as subject (*S*) and direct object (*O*) - are variously encoded in languages, the two most widespread strategies being: i) structural encoding through *word order*, and ii) morpho-syntactic marking. In turn, morpho-syntactic marking can apply either on the noun head only, in the form of *case inflections*, or on both the noun and the verb, in the form of agreement marking (Croft 2003). Besides formal coding, the distribution of subjects and object is also governed by semantic and pragmatic factors, such as noun animacy, definiteness, topicality, etc. As a result, there exists a variety of linguistic clues jointly co-operating in making a particular noun phrase the subject or direct object of a sentence. Crucially for our present purposes, cross-linguistic variation does not only concern the particular strategy used to encode *S* and *O*, but also the *relative strength* that each factor plays in a given language. For instance, while English word order is by and large the dominant clue to identify *S* and *O*, in other languages the presence of a rich morphological system allows word order to have a much looser connection with the coding of grammatical relations, thus playing a secondary role in their identification. Moreover, there are languages where semantic and pragmatic constraints such as animacy and/or definiteness play a predominant role in the processing of grammatical relations. A large spectrum of variations exists, ranging from languages where *S must* have a higher degree of animacy and/or definiteness relative to *O*, to languages where this constraint only takes the form of a softer statistical preference (cf. Bresnan *et al.* 2001).

The goal of this paper is to explore the area of this complex space of grammar variation through careful assessment of the distribution of *S* and *O* tokens in Italian and Czech. For our present analysis, we have used a MaxEnt statistical model trained on data extracted from two syntactically annotated corpora: the *Prague Dependency Treebank* (PDT, Bohmova *et al.* 2003) for Czech, and the *Italian Syntactic Semantic Treebank* (ISST, Montemagni *et al.* 2003) for Italian. These corpora have been chosen not only because they are the largest syntactically annotated resources for the two languages, but also because of their high degree of comparability, since they both adopt a dependency-based annotation scheme.

Czech and Italian provide an interesting vantage point for the cross-lingual analysis of grammatical variation. They are both Indo-European languages, but they do not belong to the same family: Czech is a West Slavonic language, while Italian is a Romance language. For our present concerns, they appear to share two crucial features: i) the free order of grammatical relations with respect to the verb; ii) the possible absence of an overt subject. Nevertheless, they also greatly differ due to: the virtual non-existence of case marking in Italian (with the only marginal exception of personal pronouns), and the degree of phrase-order freedom in the two languages. Empirical evidence supporting the latter claim is provided in Table 1, which reports data extracted from PDT and ISST. Notice that although in both languages *S* and *O* can occur either pre-verbally or post-verbally, Czech and Italian greatly differ in their propensity to depart from the (unmarked) SVO order. While in Italian preverbal *O* is highly infrequent (1.90%), in Czech more than 30% of *O* tokens occur before the verb. The situation is similar but somewhat more balanced in the case of *S*, which occurs post-verbally in 22.21% of the Italian cases, and in 40% of Czech ones. For sure, one can argue that, in spoken Italian, the number of pre-verbal objects is actually higher, because of the greater number of left dislocations and topicalizations occurring in informal speech. However reasonable, the observation does not explain away the distributional differences in the two corpora, since both PDT and ISST contain written language only. We thus suggest that there is clear empirical evidence in favour of a systematic, higher phrase-order freedom in Czech, arguably related to the well-known correlation of Czech constituent placement with sentence information structure, with the element carrying new information showing a tendency to occur sentence-finally (Stone 1990). For our present concerns, however, aspects of information structure, albeit central in Czech grammar, were not taken into account, as they happen not to be

		Czech		Italian	
		Subj	Obj	Subj	Obj
Pos	Pre	59.82%	30.27%	77.79%	1.90%
	Post	40.18%	69.73%	22.21%	98.10%
	All	100.00%	100.00%	100.00%	100.00%
Agr	Agr	98.50%	56.54%	97.73%	58.33%
	NoAgr	1.50%	43.46%	2.27%	41.67%
	All	100.00%	100.00%	100.00%	100.00%
Anim	Anim	34.10%	15.42%	50.18%	10.67%
	NoAnim	65.90%	84.58%	49.82%	89.33%
	All	100.00%	100.00%	100.00%	100.00%

Table 1 –*Distribution of Czech and Italian S and O wrt word order, agreement and noun animacy*

	Czech	
	Subj	Obj
Nominative	53.83%	0.65%
Accusative	0.15%	28.30%
Dative	0.16%	9.54%
Genitive	0.22%	2.03%
Instrumental	0.01%	3.40%
Ambiguous	45.63%	56.08%
All	100.00%	100.00%

Table 2 - *Distribution of Czech S and O wrt case*

marked-up in the Italian corpus.

According to the data reported in Table 1, Czech and Italian show similar correlation patterns between animacy and grammatical relations. *S* and *O* in ISST were automatically annotated for animacy using the SIMPLE Italian computational lexicon (Lenci *et al.* 2000) as a background semantic resource. The annotation was then checked manually. Czech *S* and *O* were annotated for animacy using Czech WordNet (Pala and Smrz 2004); it is worth remarking that in Czech animacy annotation was done only automatically, without any manual revision. Italian shows a prominent asymmetry in the distribution of animate nouns in subject and object roles: over 50% of ISST subjects are animate, while only 10% of the objects are animate. Such a trend is also confirmed in Czech – although to a lesser extent - with 34.10% of animate subjects vs. 15.42% of objects.[1] Such an overwhelming preference for animate subjects in corpus data suggests that animacy may play a very important role for *S* and *O* identification in both languages.

Corpus data also provide interesting evidence concerning the actual role of morpho-syntactic constraints in the distribution of grammatical relations. *Prima facie*, agreement and case are the strongest and most directly accessible clues for *S/O* processing, as they are marked both overtly and locally. This is also confirmed by psycholinguistic evidence, showing that subjects tend to rely on these clues to identify *S/O*. However, it should be observed that agreement can be relied upon conclusively in *S/O* processing only when a nominal constituent and a verb do not agree in number and/or person (as in *leggono il libro* '(they) read the book'). Conversely, when N and V share the same person and number, no conclusion can be drawn, as trivially shown by a sentence like *il bambino legge il libro* 'the child reads the book'. In ISST, more than 58% of *O* tokens agree with their governing V, thus being formally indistinguishable from *S* on the basis of agreement features. PDT also exhibits a similar ratio, with 56% of *O* tokens agreeing with their verb head. Analogous considerations apply to case marking, whose perceptual reliability is undermined by morphological syncretism, whereby different cases are realized through the same marker. Czech data reveal the massive extent of this phenomenon and its impact on *SOI*. As reported in Table 2, more than 56% of *O* tokens extracted from PDT are formally indistinguishable from *S* in case ending. Similarly, 45% of *S* tokens are formally indistinguishable from *O* uses on the same ground. All in all, this means that in 50% of the cases a Czech noun can not be understood as the *S/O* of a sentence by relying on overt case marking only.

To sum up, corpus data lend support to the idea that in both Italian and in Czech *SOI* is governed by a complex interplay of probabilistic constraints of a different nature (morpho-syntactic, semantic, word order, etc.) as the latter are neither singly necessary nor jointly sufficient to attack the processing task at hand. It is tempting to hypothesize that the joint distribution of these data can provide a statistically reliable basis upon which relevant probabilistic constraints are bootstrapped and combined consistently. This should be possible due to i) the different degrees of clue salience in the two languages and ii) the functional need to minimize

[1] In fact, the considerable difference in animacy distribution between the two languages might only be an artefact of the way we annotated Czech nouns semantically, on the basis of their context-free classification in the Czech WordNet.

processing ambiguity in ordinary communicative exchanges. With reference to the latter point, for example, we may surmise that a speaker will be more inclined to violate one constraint on *S/O* distribution (e.g. word order) when another clue is available (e.g. animacy) that strongly supports the intended interpretation only. The following section illustrates how a MaxEnt model can be used to model these intuitions by bootstrapping constraints and their interaction from language data.

3 Maximum Entropy modelling

The MaxEnt framework offers a mathematically sound way to build a probabilistic model for *SOI*, which combines different linguistic cues. Given a linguistic context c and an outcome $a \in A$ that depends on c, in the MaxEnt framework the conditional probability distribution $p(a|c)$ is estimated on the basis of the assumption that no *a priori* constraints must be met other than those related to a set of features $f_j(a,c)$ of c, whose distribution is derived from the training data. It can be proven that the probability distribution p satisfying the above assumption is the one with the highest entropy, is unique and has the following exponential form (Berger *et al.* 1996):

$$(1) \qquad p(a \mid c) = \frac{1}{Z(c)} \prod_{j=1}^{k} \alpha_j^{f_j(a,c)}$$

where $Z(c)$ is a normalization factor, $f_j(a,c)$ are the values of k features of the pair (a,c) and correspond to the linguistic cues of c that are relevant to predict the outcome a. Features are extracted from the training data and define the constraints that the probabilistic model p must satisfy. The parameters of the distribution $\alpha_1, \ldots, \alpha_k$ correspond to *weights* associated with the features, and determine the relevance of each feature in the overall model. In the experiments reported below feature weights have been estimated with the Generative Iterative Scaling (GIS) algorithm implemented in the AMIS software (Miyao and Tsujii 2002).

We model *SOI* as the task of predicting the correct syntactic function $\varphi \in \{subject, object\}$ of a noun occurring in a given syntactic context σ. This is equivalent to building the conditional probability distribution $p(\varphi|\sigma)$ of having a syntactic function φ in a syntactic context σ. Adopting the MaxEnt approach, the distribution p can be rewritten in the parametric form of (1), with features corresponding to the linguistic contextual cues relevant to *SOI*. The context σ is a pair $<v_\sigma, n_\sigma>$, where v_σ is the verbal head and n_σ its nominal dependent in σ. This notion of σ departs from more traditional ways of describing an *SOI* context as a triple of one verb and two nouns in a certain syntactic configuration (e.g, *SOV* or *VOS*, etc.). In fact, we assume that *SOI* can be stated in terms of the more local task of establishing the grammatical function of a noun n observed in a verb-noun pair. This simplifying assumption is consistent with the claim in MacWhinney *et al.* (1984) that *SVO* word order is actually derivative from *SV* and *VO* local patterns and downplays the role of the transitive complex construction in sentence processing. Evidence in favour of this hypothesis also comes from corpus data: for instance, in ISST complete subject-verb-object configurations represent only 26% of the cases, a small percentage if compared to the 74% of verb tokens appearing with either a subject or an object only; a similar situation can be observed in PDT where complete subject-verb-object configurations occur in only 20% of the cases. Due to the comparative sparseness of canonical *SVO* constructions in Czech and Italian, it seems more reasonable to assume that children should pay a great deal of attention to both *SV* and *VO* units as cues in sentence perception (Matthews *et al.* in press). Reconstruction of the whole lexical *SVO* pattern can accordingly be seen as the end point of an acquisition process whereby smaller units are re-analyzed as being part of more comprehensive constructions. This hypothesis is more in line with a *distributed* view of canonical constructions as derivative of more basic local positional patterns, working together to yield more complex and abstract constructions. Last but not least, assuming verb-noun pairs as the relevant context for *SOI* allows us to simultaneously model the interaction of word order variation with pro-drop.

4 Feature selection

The most important part of any MaxEnt model is the selection of the context features whose weights are to be estimated from data distributions. Our feature selection strategy is grounded on the main assumption that features should correspond to theoretically and typologically well-motivated contextual cues. This allows us to evaluate the probabilistic model also with respect to its consistency with current linguistic generalizations. In turn, the model can be used as a probe into the correspondence between theoretically motivated generalizations and usage-based empirical evidence.

Features are binary functions $f_{k_i,\varphi}$ (φ,σ), which test whether a certain cue k_i for the feature φ occurs in the context σ. For our MaxEnt model, we have selected different features types that test morpho-syntactic, syntactic, and semantic key dimensions in determining the distribution of *S* and *O*.

Morpho-syntactic features. These include N-V agreement, for Italian and Czech, and case, only for Czech. The combined use of such features allow us not only to test the impact of morpho-syntactic information on *SOI*, but also to analyze patterns of cross-lingual variation stemming from language specific morphological differences, e.g. lack of case marking in Italian.

Word order. This feature essentially test the position of the noun wrt the verb, for instance:

$$(2)\ f_{post,subj}(subj,\sigma) = \begin{cases} 1 & \textit{if noun}_{\sigma}.\textit{pos} = \textit{post} \\ 0 & \textit{otherwise} \end{cases}$$

Animacy. This is the main semantic feature, which tests whether the noun in σ is animate or inanimate (cf. section 2). The centrality of this cue for grammatical relation assignment is widely supported by typological evidence (cf. Aissen 2003, Croft 2003). The Animacy Markedness Hierarchy - representing the relative markedness of the associations between grammatical functions and animacy degrees – is actually assigned the role of a functional universal principle in grammar. The hierarchy is reported below, with each item in these scales been less marked than the elements to its right:

Animacy Markedness Hierarchy
Subj/Human > Subj/Animate > Subj/Inanimate
Obj/Inanimate > Obj/Animate > Obj/Human

Markedness hierarchies have also been interpreted as probabilistic constraints estimated from corpus data (Bresnan *et al.* 2001). In our MaxEnt model we have used a reduced version of the animacy markedness hierarchy in which human and animate nouns have been both subsumed under the general class animate.

Definiteness tests the degree of "referentiality" of the noun in a context pair σ. Like for animacy, definiteness has been claimed to be associated with grammatical functions, giving rise to the following universal markedness hierarchy Aissen (2003):

Definiteness Markedness Hierarchy
Subj/Pro > Subj/Name > Subj/Def > Subj/Indef
Obj/Indef > Obj/Def > Obj/Name > Obj/Pro

According to this hierarchy, subjects with a low degree of definiteness are more marked than subjects with a high degree of definiteness (for objects the reverse pattern holds). Given the importance assigned to the definiteness markedness hierarchy in current linguistic research, we have included the definiteness cue in the MaxEnt model. In our experiments, for Italian we have used a compact version of the definiteness scale: the definiteness cue tests whether the noun in the context pair i) is a name or a pronoun ii) has a definite article iii), has an indefinite article or iv) is a bare noun (i.e. with no article). It is worth saying that bare nouns are usually placed at the bottom end of the definiteness scale. Since in Czech there is no article, we only make a distinction between proper names and common nouns.

5 Testing the model

The Italian MaxEnt model was trained on 14,643 verb-subject/object pairs extracted from ISST. For Czech, we used a training corpus of 37,947 verb-subject/object pairs extracted from PDT. In both cases, the training set was obtained by extracting all verb-subject and verb-object dependencies headed by an active verb, with the exclusion of all cases where the position of the nominal constituent was grammatically determined (e.g. clitic objects, relative clauses). It is interesting to note that in both training sets the proportion of subjects and objects relations is nearly the same: 63.06%-65.93% verb-subject pairs and 36.94%-34.07% verb-object pairs for Italian and Czech respectively.

The test corpus consists of a set of verb-noun pairs randomly extracted from the reference Treebanks: 1,000 pairs for Italian and 1,373 for Czech. For Italian, 559 pairs contained a subject and 441 contained an object; for Czech, 905 pairs contained a subject and 468 an object. Evaluation was carried out by calculating the percentage of correctly assigned relations over the total number of test pairs (accuracy). As our model always assigns one syntactic relation to each test pair, accuracy equals both standard precision and recall.

	Czech		Italian	
	Subj	Obj	Subj	Obj
Preverb	1.99%	19.40%	0.00%	6.90%
Postverb	71.14%	7.46%	71.55%	21.55%
Anim	0.50%	3.98%	6.90%	21.55%
Inanim	72.64%	22.89%	64.66%	6.90%
Nomin	0.00%	1.00%	Na	
Genitive	0.50%	0.00%		
Dative	1.99%	0.00%		
Accus	0.00%	0.00%		
Instrum	0.00%	0.00%		
Ambig	70.65%	25.87%		
Agr	70.15%	25.87%	61.21%	12.07%
NoAgr	2.99%	0.50%	7.76%	1.72%
NAAgr	0.00%	0.50%	2.59%	14.66%

Table 3 – *Types of errors for Czech and Italian*

	Czech		Italian	
	Subj	Obj	Subj	Obj
Preverb	1.24E+00	5.40E-01	1.31E+00	2.11E-02
Postverb	8.77E-01	1.17E+00	5.39E-01	1.38E+00
Anim	1.16E+00	6.63E-01	1.28E+00	3.17E-01
Inanim	1.03E+00	9.63E-01	8.16E-01	1.23E+00
PronName	1.13E+00	7.72E-01	1.13E+00	8.05E-01
DefArt	1.05E+00	9.31E-01	1.01E+00	1.02E+00
IndefArt			6.82E-01	1.26E+00
NoArticle			9.91E-01	1.02E+00
Nomin	1.23E+00	2.22E-02	Na	
Genitive	2.94E-01	1.51E+00		
Dative	2.85E-02	1.49E+00		
Accus	8.06E-03	1.39E+00		
Instrum	3.80E-03	1.39E+00		
Agr	1.18E+00	6.67E-01	1.28E+00	4.67E-01
NoAgr	7.71E-02	1.50E+00	1.52E-01	1.58E+00
NAAgr	3.75E-01	1.53E+00	2.61E-01	1.84E+00

Table 4 - *Feature value weights in NLC for Czech and Italian*

We have assumed a baseline score of 56% for Italian and of 66% for Czech, corresponding to the result yielded by a naive model assigning to each test pair the most frequent relation in the training corpus, i.e. subject. Experiments were carried out with the general features illustrated in section 4: verb agreement, case (for Czech only), word order, noun animacy and noun definiteness.

Accuracy on the test corpus is 88.4% for Italian and 85.4% for Czech. A detailed error analysis for the two languages is reported in Table 3, showing that in both languages subject identification appears to be particularly problematic. In Czech, it appears that the prototypically mistaken subjects are post-verbal (71.14%), inanimate (72.64%), ambiguously case-marked (70.65%) and agreeing with the verb (70.15%), where reported percentages refer to the whole error set. Likewise, Italian mistaken subjects can be described thus: they typically occur in post-verbal position (71.55%), are mostly inanimate (64.66%) and agree with the verb (61.21%). Interestingly, in both languages, the highest number of errors occurs when a) N has the least prototypical syntactic and semantic properties for *O* or *S* (relative to word order and noun animacy) and b) morpho-syntactic features such as agreement and case are neutralised. This shows that MaxEnt is able to home in on the core linguistic properties that govern the distribution of *S* and *O* in Italian and Czech, while remaining uncertain in the face of somewhat peripheral and occasional cases.

A further way to evaluate the goodness of fit of our model is by inspecting the weights associated with feature values for the two languages. They are reported in Table 4, where grey cells highlight the preference of each feature value for either subject or object identification. In both languages agreement with the verb strongly relates to the subject relation. For Czech, nominative case is strongly associated with subjects while the other cases with objects. Moreover, in both languages preverbal subjects are strongly preferred over preverbal objects; animate subjects are preferred over animate objects; pronouns and proper names are typically subjects.

Let us now try to relate these feature values to the Markedness Hierarchies reported in section 4. Interestingly enough, if we rank the Italian *Anim* and *Inanim* values for subjects and objects, we observe that they distribute consistently with the *Animacy Markedness Hierarchy*: *Subj/Anim* > *Subj/Inanim* and *Obj/Inanim* > *Obj/Anim*. This is confirmed by the Czech results. Similarly, by ranking the Italian values for the definiteness features in the *Subj* column by decreasing weight values we obtain the following ordering: *PronName* > *DefArt* > *IndefArt* > *NoArt*, which nicely fits in with the *Definiteness Markedness Hierarchy* in section 4. The so-called "markedness reversal" is replicated with a good degree of approximation, if we focus on the values for the same features in the *Obj* column: the *PronName* feature represents the most marked option, followed by *IndefArt*, *DefArt* and *NoArt* (the latter two showing the same feature value). The exception here is represented by the relative ordering of *IndefArt* and *DefArt* which however show very close values. The same seems to hold for Czech, where the feature ordering for *Subj* is *PronName* > *DefArt/IndefArt/NoArt* and the reverse is observed for *Obj*.

5.1 Evaluating comparative feature salience

The relative salience of the different constraints acting on *SOI* can be inferred by comparing the weights associated with individual feature values. For instance, Goldwater and Johnson (2003) show that MaxEnt can successfully be applied to learn constraint rankings in Optimality Theory, by assuming the parameter weights $<\alpha 1, \ldots, \alpha k>$ as the ranking values of the constraints.

Table 5 illustrates the constraint ranking for the two languages, ordered by decreasing weight values for both *S* and *O*. Note that, although not all constraints are applicable in both languages, the weights associated with applicable constraints exhibit the same relative salience in Czech and Italian. This seems to suggest the existence of a rather dominant (if not universal) salience scale of *S* and *O* processing constraints, in spite of the considerable difference in the marking strategies adopted by the two languages. As the relative weight of each constraint crucially depends on its overall interaction with other constraints on a given processing task, absolute weight values can considerably vary from language to language, with a resulting impact on the distribution of *S* and *O* constructions. For example, the possibility of overtly and unambiguously marking a direct object with case inflection makes wider room for preverbal use of objects in Czech. Conversely, lack of case marking in Italian considerably limits the preverbal distribution of direct objects. This evidence, however, appears to be an epiphenomenon of the interaction of fairly stable and invariant preferences, reflecting common functional tendencies in language processing. As shown in Table 5, if constraint ranking largely confirms the interplay between animacy and word order in Italian, Czech does not contradict it but rather re-modulate it somewhat, due to the "perturbation" factors introduced by its richer battery of case markers.

6 Conclusions

Probabilistic language models, machine language learning algorithms and linguistic theorizing all appear to support a view of language processing as a process of dynamic, on-line resolution of conflicting grammatical constraints. We begin to gain considerable insights into the complex process of bootstrapping nature and behaviour of these constraints upon observing their actual distribution in perceptually salient contexts. In our view of things, this trend outlines a promising framework providing fresh support to usage-based models of language acquisition through mathematical and computational simulations. Moreover, it allows scholars to investigate patterns of cross-linguistic typological variation that crucially depend on the appropriate setting of model parameters. Finally, it promises to solve, on a principled basis, traditional performance-oriented *cruces* of grammar theorizing such as degrees of human acceptability of ill-formed grammatical constructions (Hayes 2000) and the inherently graded compositionality of linguistic constructions such as morpheme-based words and word-based phrases (Bybee 2002, Hay and Baayen 2005).

We argue that the current availability of comparable, richly annotated corpora and of mathematical tools and models for corpus exploration make time ripe for probing the space of grammatical variation, both intra- and inter-linguistically, on unprecedented levels of sophistication and granularity. All in all, we anticipate that such a convergence is likely to have a twofold impact: it is bound to shed light on the integration of performance and competence factors in language study; it will make mathematical models of language increasingly able to accommodate richer and richer language evidence, thus putting explanatory theoretical accounts to the test of a usage-based empirical verification.

In the near future, we intend to pursue two parallel lines of development. First we would like to increase the context-sensitiveness of our processing task by integrating binary grammatical constraints into the broader context of multiply conflicting grammar relations. This way, we will be in a position to capture the constraint that a (transitive) verb has at most one subject and one object, thus avoiding multiple assignment of subject (object) relations in the same context. Suppose, for example, that both nouns in a noun-noun-verb triple are amenable to a subject interpretation, but that one of them is a more likely subject than the other. Then, it is reasonable to expect the model to process the less likely subject candidate as the object of the verb in the triple. Another promising line of development is based on the observation that the order in which verb arguments appear in context is also lexically governed: in Italian, for example, report verbs show a strong tendency to select subjects post-verbally. Dell'Orletta *et al.* (2005) report a substantial improvement on the model performance on Italian *SOI* when lexical information is taken into account, as a lexicalized MaxEnt model appears to integrate general constructional and semantic biases with lexically-specific preferences. In a cross-lingual perspective, comparable evidence of lexical constraints on word order would allow us to discover language-wide invariants in the lexicon-grammar interplay.

References

Bates E., MacWhinney B., Caselli C., Devescovi A., Natale F., Venza V. 1984. A crosslinguistic study of the development of sentence interpretation strategies. *Child Development*, 55: 341-354.

Bohmova A., Hajic J., Hajicova E., Hladka B. 2003. The Prague Dependency Treebank: Three-Level Annotation Scenario, in A. Abeille (ed.) *Treebanks: Building and Using Syntactically Annotated Corpora,* Kluwer Academic Publishers, pp. 103-128.

Bybee J. 2002. Sequentiality as the basis of constituent structure. in T. Givón and B. Malle (eds.) *The Evolution of Language out of Pre-Language*, Amsterdam: John Benjamins. 107-132.

Croft W. 2003. *Typology and Universals. Second Edition*, Cambridge University Press, Cambridge.

Bresnan J., Dingare D., Manning C. D. 2001. Soft constraints mirror hard constraints: voice and person in English and Lummi. *Proceedings of the LFG01 Conference*, Hong Kong: 13-32.

Dell'Orletta F., Lenci A., Montemagni S., Pirrelli V. 2005. Climbing the path to grammar: a maximum entropy model of subject/object learning. *Proceedings of the ACL-2005 Workshop "Psychocomputational Models of Human Language Acquisition"*, University of Michigan, Ann Arbour (USA), 29-30 June 2005.

Hay J., Baayen R.H. 2005. Shifting paradigms: gradient structure in morphology, *Trends in Cognitive Sciences*, 9(7): 342-348.

Hayes B. 2000. Gradient Well-Formedness in Optimality Theory, in Joost Dekkers, Frank van der Leeuw and Jeroen van de Weijer (eds.) *Optimality Theory: Phonology, Syntax, and Acquisition*, Oxford University Press, pp. 88-120.

Lenci A. *et al.* 2000. SIMPLE: A General Framework for the Development of Multilingual Lexicons. *International Journal of Lexicography*, 13 (4): 249-263.

MacWhinney B. 2004. A unified model of language acquisition. In J. Kroll & A. De Groot (eds.), *Handbook of bilingualism: Psycholinguistic approaches*, Oxford University Press, Oxford.

Manning C. D. 2003. Probabilistic syntax. In R. Bod, J. Hay, S. Jannedy (eds), *Probabilistic Linguistics*, MIT Press, Cambridge MA: 289-341.

Miyao Y., Tsujii J. 2002. Maximum entropy estimation for feature forests. *Proc. HLT2002*.

Montemagni S. *et al.* 2003. Building the Italian syntactic-semantic treebank. In Abeillé A. (ed.) *Treebanks. Building and Using Parsed Corpora*, Kluwer, Dordrecht: 189-210.

Ratnaparkhi A. 1998. *Maximum Entropy Models for Natural Language Ambiguity Resolution*. Ph.D. Dissertation, University of Pennsylvania.

Constraints for S		
Feature	Italian	Czech
Preverbal	1.31E+00	1.24E+00
Nomin	na	1.23E+00
Agr	1.28E+00	1.18E+00
Anim	1.28E+00	1.16E+00
Inanim	8.16E-01	1.03E+00
Postverbal	5.39E-01	8.77E-01
Genitive	na	2.94E-01
NoAgr	1.52E-01	7.71E-02
Dative	na	2.85E-02
Accus	na	8.06E-03
Instrum	na	3.80E-03

Constraints for O		
Feature	Italian	Czech
Genitive	na	1.51E+00
NoAgr	1.58E+00	1.50E+00
Dative	na	1.49E+00
Accus	na	1.39E+00
Instrum	na	1.39E+00
Postverbal	1.38E+00	1.17E+00
Inanim	1.23E+00	9.63E-01
Agr	4.67E-01	6.67E-01
Anim	3.17E-01	6.63E-01
Preverbal	2.11E-02	5.40E-01
Nomin	na	2.22E-02

Table 5 – *Ranked constraints for S and O in Czech and Italian*

Frontiers in Linguistic Annotation for Lower-Density Languages

Mike Maxwell
Center for Advanced Study of Language
University of Maryland
mmaxwell@casl.umd.edu

Baden Hughes
Department of Computer Science
The University of Melbourne
badenh@csse.unimelb.edu.au

Abstract

The languages that are most commonly subject to linguistic annotation on a large scale tend to be those with the largest populations or with recent histories of linguistic scholarship. In this paper we discuss the problems associated with lower-density languages in the context of the development of linguistically annotated resources. We frame our work with three key questions regarding the definition of lower-density languages; increasing available resources and reducing data requirements. A number of steps forward are identified for increasing the number lower-density language corpora with linguistic annotations.

1 Introduction

The process for selecting a target language for research activity in corpus linguistics, natural language processing or computational linguistics is largely arbitrary. To some extent, the motivation for a specific choice is based on one or more of a range of factors: the number of speakers of a given language; the economic and social dominance of the speakers; the extent to which computational and/or lexical resources already exist; the availability of these resources in a manner conducive to research activity; the level of geopolitical support for language-specific activity, or the sensitivity of the language in the political arena; the degree to which the researchers are likely to be appreciated by the speakers of the language simply because of engagement; and the potential scientific returns from working on the language in question (including the likelihood that the language exhibits interesting or unique phenomena). Notably, these factors are also significant in determining whether a language is worked on for documentary and descriptive purposes, although an additional factor in this particular area is also the degree of endangerment (which can perhaps be contrasted with the likelihood of economic returns for computational endeavour).

As a result of these influencing factors, it is clear that languages which exhibit positive effects in one or more of these areas are likely to be the target of computational research. If we consider the availability of computationally tractable language resources, we find, unsuprisingly that major languages such as English, German, French and Japanese are dominant; and research on computational approaches to linguistic analysis tends to be farthest advanced in these languages.

However, renewed interest in the annotation of lower-density languages has arisen for a number of reasons, both theoretical and practical. In this paper we discuss the problems associated with lower-density languages in the context of the development of linguistically annotated resources.

The structure of this paper is as follows. First we define the lower-density languages and linguistically annotated resources, thus defining the scope of our interest. We review some related work in the area of linguistically annotated corpora for lower-density languages. Next we pose three questions which frame the body of this paper: What is the current status of in terms of lower-density languages which have linguistically annotated corpora? How can we more efficiently create this particular type of data for lower-density languages? Can existing analytical methods methods perform reliably with less data? A number of steps are identified for advancing the agenda of linguis-

Proceedings of the Workshop on Frontiers in Linguistically Annotated Corpora 2006, pages 29–37,
Sydney, July 2006.

tically annotated resources for lower-density languages, and finally we draw conclusions.

2 Lower-Density Languages

It should be noted from the outset that in this paper we interpret 'density' to refer to the amount of computational resources available, rather than the number of speakers any given language might have.

The fundamental problem for annotation of lower-density languages is that they are lower-density. While on the surface, this is a tautology, it in fact is the problem. For a few languages of the world (such as English, Chinese and Modern Standard Arabic, and a few Western European languages), resources are abundant; these are the high-density Languages. For a few more languages (other European languages, for the most part), resources are, if not exactly abundant, at least existent, and growing; these may be considered medium-density languages. Together, high-density and medium-density languages account for perhaps 20 or 30 languages, although of course the boundaries are arbitrary. For all other languages, resources are scarce and hence they fall into our specific area of interest.

3 Linguistically Annotated Resources

While the scarcity of language resources for lower-density languages is apparent for all resource types (with the possible exception of monolingual text), it is particularly true of linguistically annotated texts. By annotated texts, we include the following sorts of computational linguistic resources:

- Parallel text aligned with another language at the sentence level (and/or at finer levels of parallelism, including morpheme-level glossing)

- Text annotated for named entities at various levels of granularity

- Morphologically analyzed text (for non-isolating languages; at issue here is particularly inflectional morphology, and to a lesser degree of importance for most computational purposes, derivational morphology); also a morphological tag schema appropriate to the particular language

- Text marked for word boundaries (for those scripts which, like Thai, do not mark most word boundaries)

- POS tagged text, and a POS tag schema appropriate to the particular language

- Treebanked (syntactically annotated and parsed) text

- Semantically tagged text (semantic roles) cf. Propbank (Palmer et al., 2005), or frames cf. Framenet[1]

- Electronic dictionaries and other lexical resources, such as Wordnet[2]

There are numerous dimensions for linguistically annotated resources, and a range of research projects have attempted to identify the core properties of interest. While concepts such as the Basic Language Resource Kit (BLARK; (Krauwer, 2003; Mapelli and Choukri, 2003)) have gained considerable currency in higher-density language resource creation projects, it is clear that the baseline requirements of such schemes are significantly more advanced than we can hope for for lower-density languages in the short to medium term. Notably, the concept of a reduced BLARK ('BLARKette') has recently gained some currency in various forums.

4 Key Questions

Given that the vast majority of the more than seven thousand languages documented in the Ethnologue (Gordon, 2005) fall into the class of lower-density languages, what should we do? Equally important, what can we realistically do? We pose three questions by which to frame the remainder of this paper.

1. **Status Indicators**: How do we know where we are? How do we keep track of what languages are high-density or medium-density, and which are lower-density?

2. **Increasing Available Resources**: How (or can) we encourage the movement of languages up the scale from lower-density to medium-density or high-density?

[1] http://framenet.icsi.berkeley.edu/
[2] http://wordnet.princeton.edu

3. **Reducing Data Requirements**: Given that some languages will always be relatively lower-density, can language processing applications be made smarter, so that they don't require largely unattainable resources in order to perform adequately?

5 Status Indicators

We have been deliberately vague up to this point about how many lower-density languages there are, or the simpler question, how my high and medium density languages there are. Of course one reason for this is that the boundary between low density and medium or high density is inherently vague. Another reason is that the situation is constantly changing; many Central and Eastern European languages which were lower-density languages a decade or so ago are now arguably medium density, if not high density. (The standard for high vs. low density changes, too; the bar is considerably higher now than it was ten years ago.)

But the primary reason for being vague about how many – and which – languages are low density today is that no is keeping track of what resources are available for most languages. So we simply have no idea which languages are low density, and more importantly (since we can guess that in the absence of evidence to the contrary, a language is likely to be low density), we don't know which resource types most languages do or do not have.

This lack of knowledge is not for lack of trying, although perhaps we have not been trying hard enough. The following are a few of the catalogs of information about languages and their resources that are available:

- The Ethnologue[3]: This is the standard listing of the living languages of the world, but contains little or no information about what resources exist for each language.

- LDC catalog[4] and ELDA catalog[5]: The Linguistic Data Consortium (LDC) and the European Language Resources Distribution Agency (ELDA) have been among the largest distributors of annotated language data. Their catalogs, naturally, cover only those corpora distributed by each organization, and these include only a small number of languages. Naturally, the economically important languages constitute the majority of the holdings of the LDC and ELDA.

- AILLA (Archive of the Indigenous Languages of Latin America[6]), and numerous other language archiving sites: Such sites maintain archives of linguistic data for languages, often with a specialization, such as indigenous languages of a country or region. The linguistic data ranges from unannotated speech recordings to morphologically analyzed texts glossed at the morpheme level.

- OLAC (Open Archives Language Community[7]): Given that many of the above resources (particularly those of the many language archives) are hard to find, OLAC is an attempt to be a meta-catalog (or aggregator)of such resources. It allows lookup of data by type, language etc. for all data repositories that 'belong to' OLAC. In fact, all the above resources are listed in the OLAC union catalogue.

- Web-based catalogs of additional resources: There is a huge number of additional websites which catalog information about languages, ranging from electronic and print dictionaries (e.g. yourDictionary[8]), to discussion groups about particular languages[9]. Most such sites do little vetting of the resources, and dead links abound. Nevertheless, such sites (or a simple search with an Internet search engine) can often turn up useful information (such as grammatical descriptions of minority languages). Very few of these web sites are cataloged in OLAC, although recent efforts (Hughes et al., 2006a) are slowly addressing the inclusion of web-based low density language resources in such indexes.

None of the above catalogs is in any sense complete, and indeed the very notion of completeness is moot when it comes to cataloging Internet resources. But more to the point of this paper, it

[3]http://www.ethnologue.org
[4]http://www.ldc.upenn.edu/Catalog/
[5]http://www.elda.org/rubrique6.html
[6]http://www.ailla.utexas.org
[7]http://www.language-archives.org
[8]http://www.yourdictionary.com
[9]http://dir.groups.yahoo.com/dir/Cultures__Community/By_Language

is difficult, if not impossible, to get a picture of the state of language resources in general. How many languages have sufficient bitext (and in what genre), for example, that one could put together a statistical machine translation system? What languages have morphological parsers (and for what languages is such a parser more or less irrelevant, because the language is relatively isolating)? Where can one find character encoding converters for the Ge'ez family of fonts for languages written in Ethiopic script?

The answer to such questions is important for several reasons:

1. If there were a crisis that involved an arbitrary language of the world, what resources could be deployed? An example of such a situation might be another tsunami near Indonesia, which could affect dozens, if not hundreds of minority languages. (The December 26, 2004 tsunami was particularly felt in the Aceh province of Indonesia, where one of the main languages is Aceh, spoken by three million people. Aceh is a lower-density language.)

2. Which languages could, with a relatively small amount of effort, move from lower-density status to medium-density or high-density status? For example, where parallel text is harvestable, a relatively small amount of work might suffice to produce many applications, or other resources (e.g. by projecting syntactic annotation across languages). On the other hand, where the writing system of a language is in flux, or the language is politically oppressed, a great deal more effort might be necessary.

3. For which low density languages might related languages provide the leverage needed to build at least first draft resources? For example, one might think of using Turkish (arguably at least a medium-density language) as a sort of pivot language to build lexicons and morphological parsers for such low density Turkic languages as Uzbek or Uyghur.

4. For which low density languages are there extensive communities of speakers living in other countries, who might be better able to build language resources than speakers living in the perhaps less economically developed home countries? (Expatriate communities may also be motivated by a desire to maintain their language among younger speakers, born abroad.)

5. Which languages would require more work (and funding) to build resources, but are still plausible candidates for short term efforts?

To our knowledge, there is no general, on-going effort to collect the sort of data that would make answers to these questions possible. A survey was done at the Linguistic Data Consortium several years ago (Strassel et al., 2003) , for text-based resources for the three hundred or so languages having at least a million speakers (an arbitrary cutoff, to be sure, but necessary for the survey to have had at least some chance of success). It was remarkably successful, considering that it was done by two linguists who did not know the vast majority of the languages surveyed. The survey was funded long enough to 'finish' about 150 languages, but no subsequent update was ever done.

A better model for such a survey might be an edited book: one or more computational linguists would serve as 'editors', responsible for the overall framework, and training of other participants. Section 'editors' would be responsible for a language family, or for the languages of a geographic region or country. Individual language experts would receive a small amount of training to enable them to answer the survey questions for their language, and then paid to do the initial survey, plus periodic updates. The model provided by the Ethnologue (Gordon, 2005) may serve as a starting point, although for the level of detail that would be useful in assessing language resource availability will make wholesale adoption unsuitable.

6 Increasing Available Resources

Given that a language significantly lacks computational linguistic resources (and in the context of this paper and the associated workshop, annotated text resources), so that it falls into the class of lower-density languages (however that might be defined), what then?

Most large-scale collections of computational linguistics resources have been funded by government agencies, either the US government (typically the Department of Defense) or by governments of countries where the languages in question are spoken (primarily European, but also a few other financially well-off countries). In some cases, governments have sponsored collections for languages which are not indigenous to the country in question (e.g. the EMILLE project[10], see (McEnery et al., 2000)).

In most such projects, production of resources for lower-density languages have been the work of a very small team which oversees the effort, together with paid annotators and translators. More specifically, collection and processing of monolingual text can be done by a linguist who need not know the language (although it helps to have a speaker of the language who can be called on to do language identification, etc.). Dictionary collection from on-line dictionaries can also be done by a linguist; but if it takes much more effort than that – for example, if the dictionary needs to be converted from print format to electronic format – it is again preferable to have a language speaker available.

Annotating text (e.g. for named entities) is different: it can only be done by a speaker of the language (more accurately, a reader: for Punjabi, for instance, it can be difficult to find fluent readers of the Gurmukhi script). Preferably the annotator is familiar enough with current events in the country where the language is spoken that they can interpret cross-references in the text. If two or more annotators are available, the work can be done somewhat more quickly. More importantly, there can be some checking for inter-annotator agreement (and revision taking into account such differences as are found).

Earlier work on corpus collection from the web (e.g. (Resnik and Smith, 2003)) gave some hope that reasonably large quantities of parallel text could be found on the web, so that a bitext collection could be built for interesting language pairs (with one member of the pair usually being English) relatively cheaply. Subsequent experience with lower-density languages has not born that hope out; parallel text on the web seems relatively rare for most languages. It is unclear why this should be. Certainly in countries like India, there are large amounts of news text in English and many of the target languages (such as Hindi). Nevertheless, very little of that text seems to be genuinely parallel, although recent work (Munteanu and Marcu, 2005) indicates that true parallelism may not be required for some tasks, eg machine translation, in order to gain acceptable results.

Because bitext was so difficult to find for lower-density languages, corpus creation efforts rely largely, if not exclusively, on contracting out text for translation. In most cases, source text is harvested from news sites in the target language, and then translated into English by commercial translation agencies, at a rate usually in the neighborhood of US$0.25 per word. In theory, one could reduce this cost by dealing directly with translators, avoiding the middleman agencies. Since many translators are in the Third World, this might result in considerable cost savings. Nevertheless, quality control issues loom large. The more professional agencies do quality control of their translations; even so, one may need to reject translations in some cases (and the agencies themselves may have difficulty in dealing with translators for languages for which there is comparatively little demand). Obviously this overall cost is high; it means that a 100k word quantity of parallel text will cost in the neighborhood of US$25K.

Other sources of parallel text might include government archives (but apart from parliamentary proceedings where these are published bilingually, such as the Hansards, these are usually not open), and the archives of translation companies (but again, these are seldom if ever open, because the agencies must guard the privacy of those who contracted the translations).

Finally, there is the possibility that parallel text – and indeed, other forms of annotation – could be produced in an open source fashion. Wikipedia[11] is perhaps the most obvious instance of this, as there are parallel articles in English and other languages. Unfortunately, the quantity of such parallel text at the Wikipedia is very small for all but a few languages. At present (May 2006), there are over 100,000 articles in German, Spanish, French, Italian, Japanese, Dutch, Polish, Portuguese and Swedish.[12] Languages with over 10,000 articles include Arabic, Bulgarian, Catalan, Czech, Danish, Estonian, Esperanto and Ido (both constructed languages), Persian, Galician, Hebrew, Croatian), Bahasa Indonesian, Korean, Lithuanian, Hungarian, Bahasa Malay, Norwegian

[10]http://bowland-files.lancs.ac.uk/corplang/emille/

[11]http://en.wikipedia.org

[12]Probably some of these articles are non-parallel. Indeed, a random check of Cebuano articles in Wikipedia revealed that many were stubs (a term used in the Wikipedia to refer to "a short article in need of expansion"), or were simply links to Internet blogs, many of which were monolingual in English.

(Bokmål and Nynorsk), Romanian, Russian, Slovak, Slovenian, Serbian, Finnish, Thai, Turkish, Ukrainian, and Chinese. The dominance of European languages in these lists is obvious.

During a TIDES exercise in 2003, researchers at Johns Hopkins University explored an innovative approach to the creation of bitext (parallel English and Hindi text, aligned at the sentence level): they elicited translations into English of Hindi sentences they posted on an Internet web page (Oard, 2003; Yarowsky, 2003). Participants were paid for the best translations in Amazon.com gift certificates, with the quality of a twenty percent subset of the translations automatically evaluated using BLEU scores against highly scored translations of the same sentences from previous rounds. This pool of high-quality translations was initialized to a set of known quality translations. A valuable side effect of the use of previously translated texts for evaluation is that this created a pool of multiply translated texts.

The TIDES translation exercise quickly produced a large body of translated text: 300K words, in five days, at a cost of about two cents per word.

This approach to resource creation is similar to numerous open source projects, in the sense that the work is being done by the public. It differed in that the results of this work were not made publicly available; the use of an explicit quality control method; and of course the payments to (some) participants. While the quality control aspect may be essential to producing useful language resources, hiding those resources not currently being used for evaluation is not essential to the methodology.

Open source resource creation efforts are of course common, with the Wikipedia[13] being the best known. Other such projects include Amazon.com's Mechanical Turk[14], LiTgloss[15], The ESP Game[16], and the Wiktionary[17]. Clearly some forms of annotation will be easier to do using an open source methodology than others will. For example, translation and possibly named entity annotation might be fairly straightforward, while morphological analysis is probably more difficult, particularly for morphologically complex languages.

[13]http://www.wikipedia.org

[14]http://www.mturk.com/mturk/

[15]http://litgloss.buffalo.edu/

[16]http://www.espgame.org/

[17]http://wiktionary.org/

Other researchers have experimented with the automatic creation of corpora using web data (Ghani et al., 2001) Some of these corpora have grown to reasonable sizes; (Scannell, 2003; Scannell, 2006) has corpora derived from web crawling which are measured in tens of millions of words for a variety of lower-density languages. However it should be noted that in these cases, the type of linguistic resource created is often not linguistically annotated, but rather a lexicon or collection of primary texts in a given language.

Finally, we may mention efforts to create certain kinds of resources by computer-directed elicitation. Examples of projects sharing this focus include BOAS (Nirenburg and Raskin, 1998), and the AVENUE project (Probst et al., 2002), (Lavie et al., 2003).

7 Reducing Data Requirements

Creating more annotated resources is the obvious way to approach the problem of the lack of resources for lower-density languages. A complementary approach is to improve the way the information in smaller resources is used, for example by developing machine translation systems that require less parallel text.

How much reduction in the required amount of resources might be enough? An interesting experiment, which to our knowledge has never been tried, would be for a linguist to attempt as a test case what we hope that computers can do. That is, a linguist could take a 'small' quantity of parallel text, and extract as much lexical and grammatical information from that as possible. The linguist might then take a previously unseen text in the target language and translate it into English, or perform some other useful task on target language texts. One might argue over whether this experiment would constitute an upper bound on how much information could be extracted, but it would probably be more information than current computational approaches extract.

Naturally, this approach partially shifts the problem from the research community interested in linguistically annotated corpora to the research community interested in algorithms. Much effort has been invested in scaling algorithmic approaches upwards, that is, leveraging every last available data point in pursuit of small performance improvements. We argue that scaling down (ie using less training data) poses an equally significant challenge. The basic question of whether methods which are data-rich can scale down to impoverished data has been the focus of a number of recent papers in areas such as machine translation (Somers, 1997; Somers, 1998), language identification (Hughes et al., 2006b) etc. However, tasks which have lower-density language at their core have yet to become mainstream in shared evaluation tasks which drive much of the algorithmic improvements in computational linguistics and natural language processing.

Another approach to data reduction is to change the type of data required for a given task. For many lower-density languages a significant volume of linguistically annotated data exists, but not in the form of the curated, standardised corpora to which language technologists are accustomed. Neverthless for extremely low density languages, a degree of standardisation is apparent by virtue of documentary linguistic practice. Consider for example, the number of Shoebox lexicons and corresponding interlinear texts which are potentially available from documentary sources: while not being the traditional resource types on which systems are trained, they are reasonably accessible, and cover a larger number of languages. Bible translations are another form of parallel text available in nearly every written language (see (Resnik et al., 1999)). There are of course issues of quality, not to mention vocabulary, that arise from using the Bible as a source of parallel text, but for some purposes – such as morphology learning – Bible translations might be a very good source of data.

Similarly, a different compromise may be found in the ratio of the number of words in a corpus to the richness of linguistic annotation. In many high-density corpora development projects, an arbitrary (and high) target for the number of words is often set in advance, and subsequent linguistic annotation is layered over this base corpus in a progressively more granular fashion. It may be that this corpus development model could be modified for lower-density language resource development: we argue that in many cases, the richness of linguistic annotation over a given set of data is more important than the raw quantity of the data set.

A related issue is different standards for annotating linguistic concepts We already see this in larger languages (consider the difference in morpho-syntactic tagging between the Penn Treebank and other corpora), but has there is a higher diversity of standards in lower-density languages. Solutions may include ontologies for linguistic concepts e.g. General Ontology for Linguistic Description[18] and the ISO Data Category Registry (Ide and Romary, 2004), which allow cross-resource navigation based on common semantics. Of course, cross-language and cross-cultural semantics is a notoriously difficult subject.

Finally, it may be that development of web based corpora can act as the middle ground: there are plenty of documents on the web in lower-density languages, and efforts such as projects by Scannell[19] and Lewis[20] indicate these can be curated reasonably efficiently, even though the outcomes may be slightly different to that which we are accustomed. Is it possible to make use of XML or HTML markup directly in these cases? Someday, the semantic web may help us with this type of approach.

8 Moving Forward

Having considered the status of linguistically-annotated resources for lower-density languages, and two broad strategies for improving this situation (innovative approaches to data creation, and scaling down of resource requirements for existing techniques), we now turn to the question of where to go from here. We believe that there are a number of practical steps which can be taken in order to increase the number of linguistically-annotated lower-density language resources available to the research community:

- Encouraging the publication of electronic corpora of lower-density languages: most economic incentives for corpus creation only exhibit return on investment because of the focus on higher-density languages; new models of funding and commercializing corpora for lower-density languages are required.

- Engaging in research on bootstrapping from higher density language resources to lower-density surrogates: it seems obvious that at least for related languages adopting a derivational approach to the generation of linguistically annotated corpora for lower-density languages by using automated annotation tools trained on higher-density lan-

[18]http://www.linguistics-ontology.org
[19]http://borel.slu.edu/crubadan/stadas.html
[20]http://www.csufresno.edu/odin

guages may at least reduce the human effort required.

- Scaling down (through data requirement reduction) of state of the art algorithms: there has been little work in downscaling state of the art algorithms for tasks such as named entity recognition, POS tagging and syntactic parsing, yet (considerably) reducing the training data requirement seems like one of the few ways that existing analysis technologies can be applied to lower-density languages.

- Shared evaluation tasks which include lower-density languages or smaller amounts of data: most shared evaluation tasks are construed as exercises in cross-linguistic scalability (eg CLEF) or data intensivity (eg TREC) or both (eg NTCIR). Within these constructs there is certainly room for the inclusion of lower-density languages as targets, although notably the overhead here is not in the provision of the language data, but the derivatives (eg query topics) on which these exercises are based.

- Promotion of multilingual corpora which include lower-density languages: as multilingual corpora emerge, there is opportunity to include lower-density languages at minimal opportunity cost e.g. EuroGOV (Sigurbjönsson et al., 2005) or JRC-Acquis (Steinberger et al., 2006), which are based on web data from the EU, includes a number of lower-density languages by virtue of the corpus creation mechanism not being language-specific.

- Language specific strategies: collectively we have done well at developing formal strategies for high density languages e.g. in EU roadmaps, but not so well at strategies for medium-density or lower-density languages. The models for medium to long term strategies of language resource development may be adopted for lower density languages. Recently this has been evidenced through events such as the LREC 2006 workshop on African language resources and the development of a corresponding roadmap.

- Moving towards interoperability between annotation schemes which dominate the higher-density languages (eg Penn Treebank tagging conventions) and the relatively ad-hoc schemes often exhibited by lower-density languages, through means such as markup ontologies like the General Ontology for Linguistic Description or the ISO Data Category Registry.

Many of these steps are not about to be realised in the short term. However, developing a cohesive strategy for addressing the need for linguistically annotated corpora is a first step in ensuring committment from interested researchers to a common roadmap.

9 Conclusion

It is clear that the number of linguistically-annotated resources for any language will inevitably be less than optimal. Regardless of the density of the language under consideration, the cost of producing linguistically annotated corpora of a substantial size is significant, Inevitably, languages which do not have a strong political, economic or social status will be less well resourced.

Certain avenues of investigation e.g. collecting language specific web content, or building approximate bitexts web data are being explored, but other areas (such as rich morphosyntactic annotation) are not particularly evidenced.

However, there is considerable research interest in the development of linguistically annotated resources for languages of lower density. We are encouraged by the steady rate at which academic papers emerge reporting the development of resources for lower-density language targets. We have proposed a number of steps by which the issue of language resources for lower-density languages may be more efficiently created and look forward with anticipation as to how these ideas motivate future work.

References

Rayid Ghani, Rosie Jones, and Dunja Mladenic. 2001. Mining the web to create minority language corpora. In *Proceedings of 2001 ACM International Conference on Knowledge Management (CIKM2001)*, pages 279–286. Association for Computing Machinery.

Raymond G. Gordon. 2005. *Ethnologue: Languages of the World (15th Edition)*. SIL International: Dallas.

Baden Hughes, Timothy Baldwin, and Steven Bird. 2006a. Collecting low-density language data on the web. In *Proceedings of the 12th Australasian Web Conference (AusWeb06)*. Southern Cross University.

Baden Hughes, Timothy Baldwin, Steven Bird, Jeremy Nicholson, and Andrew MacKinlay. 2006b. Reconsidering language identification for written language resources. In *Proceedings of the 5th International Conference on Language Resources and Evaluation (LREC2006)*. European Language Resources Association: Paris.

Nancy Ide and Laurent Romary. 2004. A registry of standard data categories for linguistic annotation. In *Proceedings of the 4th International Conference on Language Resources and Evaluation (LREC2004*, pages 135–139. European Language Resources Association: Paris.

Steven Krauwer. 2003. The basic language resource kit (BLARK) as the first milestone for the language resources roadmap. In *Proceedings of 2nd International Conference on Speech and Computer (SPECOM2003)*.

A. Lavie, S. Vogel, L. Levin, E. Peterson, K. Probst, A. Font Llitjos, R. Reynolds, J. Carbonell, and R. Cohen. 2003. Experiments with a hindi-to-english transfer-based mt system under a miserly data scenario. *ACM Transactions on Asian Language Information Processing (TALIP)*, 2(2).

Valerie Mapelli and Khalid Choukri. 2003. Report on a monimal set of language resources to be made available for as many languages as possible, and a map of the actual gaps. ENABLER internal project report (Deliverable 5.1).

Tony McEnery, Paul Baker, and Lou Burnard. 2000. Corpus resources and minority language engineering. In *Proceedings of the 2nd International Conference on Language Resources and Evaluation (LREC2002)*. European Language Resources Association: Paris.

Dragos Stefan Munteanu and Daniel Marcu. 2005. Improving machine translation performance by exploiting non-parallel corpora. *Computational Linguistics*, 31(4):477–504.

Sergei Nirenburg and Victor Raskin. 1998. Universal grammar and lexis for quick ramp-up of mt. In *Proceedings of 36th Annual Meeting of the Association for Computational Linguistics and 17th International Conference on Computational Linguistics*, pages 975–979. Association for Computational Linguistics.

Douglas W. Oard. 2003. The surprise language exercises. *ACM Transactions on Asian Language Information Processing (TALIP)*, 2(2):79–84.

Martha Palmer, Dan Gildea, and Paul Kingsbury. 2005. The proposition bank: A corpus annotated with semantic roles. *Computational Linguistics*, 31(1).

K. Probst, L. Levin, E. Peterson, A. Lavie, and J. Carbonell. 2002. Mt for minority languages using elicitation-based learning of syntactic transfer rules. *Machine Translation*, 17(4):245–270.

Philip Resnik and Noah A. Smith. 2003. The web as a parallel corpus. *Computational Linguistics*, 29(3):349–380.

Philip Resnik, Mari Broman Olsen, and Mona Diab. 1999. The Bible as a parallel corpus: Annotating the 'Book of 2000 Tongues'. *Computers and the Humanities*, 33(1-2):129–153.

Kevin Scannell. 2003. Automatic thesaurus generation for minority languages: an irish example. In *Actes des Traitement Automatique des Langues Minoritaires et des Petites Langues*, volume 2, pages 203–212.

Kevin Scannell. 2006. Machine translation for closely related language pairs. In *Proceedings of the LREC2006 Workshop on Strategies for developing machine translation for minority languages*. European Language Resources Association: Paris.

B. Sigurbjönsson, J. Kamps, and M. de Rijke. 2005. Blueprint of a cross-lingual web collection. *Journal of Digital Information Management*, 3(1):9–13.

Harold Somers. 1997. Machine translation and minority languages. *Translating and the Computer*, 19:1–13.

Harold Somers. 1998. Language resources and minority languages. *Language Today*, 5:20–24.

R. Steinberger, B. Pouliquen, A. Widger, C. Ignat, T. Erjavec, D. Tufis, and D. Varga. 2006. The jrc-acquis: A multilingual aligned parallel corpus with 20+ languages. In *Proceedings of the 5th International Conference on Language Resources and Evaluation (LREC2006)*. European Language Resources Association: Paris.

Stephanie Strassel, Mike Maxwell, and Christopher Cieri. 2003. Linguistic resource creation for research and technology development: A recent experiment. *ACM Transactions on Asian Language Information Processing (TALIP)*, 2(2):101–117.

David Yarowsky. 2003. Scalable elicitation of training data for machine translation. *Team Tides*, 4.

10 Acknowledgements

The authors are grateful to Kathryn L. Baker for her comments on earlier drafts of this paper.

Portions of the research in this paper were supported by the Australian Research Council Special Research Initiative (E-Research) grant number SR0567353 "An Intelligent Search Infrastructure for Language Resources on the Web."

Annotation Compatibility Working Group Report*

Contributors: A. Meyers, A. C. Fang, L. Ferro, S. Kübler, T. Jia-Lin, M. Palmer, M. Poesio, A. Dolbey, K. K. Schuler, E. Loper, H. Zinsmeister, G. Penn, N. Xue, E. Hinrichs, J. Wiebe, J. Pustejovsky, D. Farwell, E. Hajicova, B. Dorr, E. Hovy, B. A. Onyshkevych, L. Levin
Editor: A Meyers meyers@cs.nyu.edu

*As this report is a compilation, some sections may not reflect the views of individual contributors.

Abstract

This report explores the question of compatibility between annotation projects including translating annotation formalisms to each other or to common forms. Compatibility issues are crucial for systems that use the results of multiple annotation projects. We hope that this report will begin a concerted effort in the field to track the compatibility of annotation schemes for part of speech tagging, time annotation, treebanking, role labeling and other phenomena.

1. Introduction

Different corpus annotation projects are driven by different goals, are applied to different types of data (different genres, different languages, etc.) and are created by people with different intellectual backgrounds. As a result of these and other factors, different annotation efforts make different underlying theoretical assumptions. Thus, no annotation project is really theory-neutral, and in fact, none should be. It is the theoretical concerns which make it possible to write the specifications for an annotation project and which cause the resulting annotation to be consistent and thus usable for various natural language processing (NLP) applications. Of course the theories chosen for annotation projects tend to be theories that are useful for NLP. They place a high value on descriptive adequacy (they cover the data), they are formalized sufficiently for consistent annotation to be possible, and they tend to share major theoretical assumptions with other annotation efforts, e.g., the noun is the head of the noun phrase, the verb is the head of the sentence, etc. Thus the term *theory-neutral* is often used to mean something like *NLP-friendly*. Obviously, the annotation compatibility problem that we address here is much simpler than it would be if we had to consider theories which place a low emphasis on NLP-friendly properties (Minimalism. Optimality Theory, etc.).

As annotation projects are usually research efforts, the inherent theoretical differences may be viewed as part of a search for the truth and the enforcement of adherence to a given (potentially wrong) theory could hamper this search. In addition, annotation of particular phenomena may be simplified by making theoretical assumptions conducive to describing those phenomena. For example, relative pronouns (e.g., *that* in the NP *the book that she read*) may be viewed as pronouns in an anaphora annotation project, but as intermediate links to arguments for a study of predicate argument structure.

On the other hand, many applications would benefit by merging the results of different annotation projects. Thus, differences between annotation projects may be viewed as obstacles. For example, combining two or more corpora annotated with the same information may improve a system (i.e., "there's no data like more data.") To accomplish this, it may be necessary to convert corpora annotated according to one set of specifications into a different system or to convert two annotation systems into a third system. For example, to obtain lots of part of speech data for English, it is advantageous to convert POS tags from several tagsets (see Section 2) into a common form. For more temporal data than is available in Timex3 format, one might have to convert Timex2 and Timex3 tags into a common form (See Section 5). Compromises that do not involve conversion can be flawed. For example, a machine learner may determine that feature A in framework 1 predicts feature A' in framework 2. However, the system may miss that features A and B in framework 1 actually both correspond to feature A', i.e., they are subtypes. In our view, directly modeling the parameters of compatibility would be preferable.

Proceedings of the Workshop on Frontiers in Linguistically Annotated Corpora 2006, pages 38–53,
Sydney, July 2006. ©2006 Association for Computational Linguistics

Some researchers have attempted to combine a number of different resource annotations into a single merged form. One motivation is that the merged representation may be more than the sum of its parts. It is likely that inconsistencies and errors (often induced by task-specific biases) can be identified and adjusted in the merging process; inferences may be drawn from how the component annotation systems interact; a complex annotation in a single framework may be easier for a system to process than several annotations in different frameworks; and a merged framework will help guide further annotation research (Pustojevsky, et. al. 2005). Another reason to merge is that a merged resource in language *A* may be similar to an existing resource in language *B*. Thus merging resources may present opportunities for constructing nearly parallel resources, which in turn could prove useful for a multilingual application. Merging PropBank (Kingsbury, and Palmer 2002) and NomBank (Meyers, et. al. 2004) would yield a predicate argument structure for nouns and verbs, carrying more similar information to the Praque Dependency TreeBank's TectoGrammatical structure (Hajicova and Ceplova, 2000) than either component.

This report and an expanded online version http://nlp.cs.nyu.edu/wiki/corpuswg/AnnotationCompatibility both describe how to find correspondences between annotation frameworks. This information can be used to combine various annotation resources in different ways, according to one's research goals, and, perhaps, could lead to some standards for combining annotation. This report will outline some of our initial findings in this effort with an eye towards maintaining and updating the online version in the future. We hope this is a step towards making it easier for systems to use multiple annotation resources.

2. Part of Speech and Phrasal Categories

On our website, we provide correspondences among a number of different part of speech tagsets in a version of the table from pp. 141--142 of Manning and Schütze (1999), modified to include the POS classes from CLAWS1 and ICE. Table 1 is a sample taken from this table for expository purposes (the full table is not provided due to space limitations). Traditionally, part of speech represents a fairly coarse-grained division among types of words, usually distinguishing among: nouns, verbs, adjectives, adverbs, determiners and possibly a few other classes. While part of speech classifications may vary for particular words, especially closed class items, we have observed a larger problem. Most part of speech annotation projects incorporate other distinctions into part of speech classification. Furthermore, they incorporate different types of distinctions. As a result, conversion between one tagset and another is rarely one to one. It can, in fact, be many to many, e.g., BROWN does not distinguish the

Table 1: Part of Speech Compatibility

Extending Manning and Schütze 1999, pp. 141-142, to cover Claws1 and ICE -- Longer Version Online

Class	Wrds	Claws c5, Claws1	Brown	PTB	ICE
Adj	Hap-py, bad	AJ0	JJ	JJ	ADJ. ge
Adj, comp	hap-pier, worse	AJC	JJR	JJR	ADJ. comp
Adj, super	nic-est-worst	AJS	JJT	JJS	ADJ. sup
Adj, past part	eaten	JJ	??	VBN, JJ	ADJ. edp
Adj, pres part	calm-ing	JJ	??	VBG, JJ	ADJ. ingp
Adv	slow-ly, sweet-ly	AV0	RB	RB	ADV. ge
Adv comp	faster	AV0	RBR	RBR	ADV. comp
Adv super	fast-est	AV0	RBT	RBS	ADV. sup
Adv Part	up, off, out	AVP, RP, RI	RP	RP	ADV. {phras, ge}
Conj coord	and, or	CJC, CC	CC	CC	CON-JUNC.

					coord
Det	this, each, another	DT0, DT	DT	DT	PRON. dem.sing, PRON (recip)
Det. pron	any, some	DT0, DTI	DT1	DT	PRON. nonass, PRON. ass
Det pron Plur	these those	DT0, DTS	DTS	DT	PRON. dem. plu
Det preq	quite	DT0, aBL	ABL	PDT	ADV .intens
Det preq	all, half	DT0, ABN	ABN	PDT	PRON. univ, PRON. quant
Noun	air-craft, data	NN0	NN	NN	N.com. sing
Noun sing	cat, pen	NN1	NN	NN	N.com. sing
Noun plur	cats, pens	NN2	NNS	NNS	N.com. plu
Noun prop sing	Paris, Mike	NP0	NP	NNP	N.prop .sing
Verb. base pres	take, live	VVB	VB	VBP	V.X. {pres, imp}
Verb, infin	take, live	VVI	VB	VB	V.X. infin
Verb, past	took, lived	VVD	VBD	VBD	V.X. past
Verb, pres part	taking, living	VVG	VBG	VBG	V.X. ingp
Verb, past-part	taken, lived	VVN	VBN	VBN	V.X. edp
Verb, pres	takes,	VVZ	VBZ	VBZ	V.X. pres

infinitive form of a verb (VB in the Penn Treebank, V.X.infin in ICE) from the present-tense form (VBP in the Penn Treebank, V.X.pres in ICE) that has the same spelling (e.g., *see* in *They see no reason to leave*). In contrast, ICE distinguishes among several different subcategories of verb (cop, intr, cxtr, dimontr, ditr, montr and TRANS) and the Penn Treebank does not.[1] In a hypothetical system which merges all the different POS tagsets, it would be advantageous to factor out different types of features (similar to ICE), but include all the distinctions made by all the tag sets. For example, if a token *give* is tagged as VBP in the Penn Treebank, VBP would be converted into VERB.anysubc.pres. If another token *give* was tagged VB in Brown, VB would be converted to VERB.anysubc{infin,n3pres} (n3pres = not-3rd-person and present tense). This allows systems to acquire the maximum information from corpora, tagged by different research groups.

CKIP Chinese-Treebank (CCTB) and Penn Chinese Treebank (PCTB) are two important resources for Treebank-derived Chinese NLP tasks (CKIP, 1995; Xia et al., 2000; Xu et al., 2002; Li et al., 2004). CCTB is developed in traditional Chinese (BIG5-encoded) at the Academia Sinica, Taiwan (Chen et al., 1999; Chen et al., 2003). CCTB uses the Information-based Case Grammar (ICG) framework to express both syntactic and semantic descriptions. The present version CCTB3 (Version 3) provides 61,087 Chinese sentences, 361,834 words and 6 files that are bracketed and post-edited by humans based on a 5-million-word tagged Sinica Corpus (CKIP, 1995). CKIP POS tagging is a hierarchical system. The first POS layers include eight main syntactic categories, i.e. **N** (noun), **V** (verb), **D** (adverb), **A** (adjective), **C** (conjunction), **I** (interjection), **T** (particles) and **P** (preposition). In CCTB, there are 6 non-terminal phrasal categories: **S** (a complete tree headed by a predicate), **VP** (a phrase headed by a predicate), **NP** (a phrase beaded by an N), **GP** (a phrase headed by locational noun or adjunct), **PP**

[1] In the ICE column of Table 1 X represents the disjunction of verb subcategorization types {cop, intr, cxtr, dimontr, ditr, montr, trans}.

(a phrase headed by a preposition) and **XP** (a conjunctive phrase that is headed by a conjunction).

Examples	Top Layer (TL)		Bottom Layer (BL)	
	PCTB	CCTB	PCTB	CCTB
換句話說 in other words	ADVP	Head	AD	Dk
於是 therefore	ADVP	result	AD	Cbca
因為 because	P	reason	P	Cbaa
過去 past	NP-TMP	time:NP	NT	Ndda
去年 last year	NP-TMP	NP	NT	Ndaba
其中 among	NP-ADV	NP	NN	Nep
同樣地 also	DVP	ADV	AD:DEV	Dk
近年來 in the last few years	LCP-TMP	GP	NT:LCGP	Nddc:Ng

PCTB annotates simplified Chinese texts (GB-encoded) from newswire sources (Xinhua newswire, Hong Kong news and Sinorama news magazine, Taiwan). It is developed at the University of Pennsylvania (UPenn). The PCTB annotates Chinese texts with syntactic bracketing, part of speech information, empty categories and function tags (Xia et al, 2000, 2002, 2005). The predicate-argument structure of Chinese verbs for the PCTB is encoded in the Penn Chinese Proposition Bank (Xue, et. Al. 2005). The present version PCTB5.1 (PCTB Version 5.1), contains 18,782 sentences, 507,222 words, 824,983 Hanzi and 890 data files. PCTB's bracketing annotation is in the same framework as other Penn Treebanks, bearing a loose connection to the Government and Binding Theory paradigm. The PCTB annotation scheme involves 33 POS-tags, 17 phrasal tags, 6 verb compound tags, 7 empty category tags and 26 functional tags.

Table 2 includes Top-Layer/Bottom-Layer POS and phrasal categories correspondences between PCTB4 and CCTB3 for words/phrases expressed as the same Chinese characters in the same order.

3. Differences Between Frameworks

We assume that certain high level differences between annotation schemata should be ignored if at all possible, namely those that represent differences of analyses that are notationally equivalent. In this section, we will discuss those sorts of differences with an eye towards evaluating whether real differences do in fact exist, so that way users of annotation can be careful should these differences be of significance to their particular application.

To clarify, we are talking about the sort of high level differences which reflect differences in the linguistic framework used for representing annotation, e.g., many frameworks represent long distance dependencies in equivalent, but different ways. In this sense, the linguistic framework of the Penn Treebank is a phrase structure based framework that includes a particular set of node labels (POS tags, phrasal categories, etc.), function tags, indices, etc. [2].

3.1 Dependency vs. Constituency

Figure 1 is a candidate rule for converting a phrase structure tree to a dependency tree or vice versa. Given a phrase consisting of constituents C(n-i) to C(n+j), the rule assumes that: there is one unique constituent C(n) that is the head of the phrase; and it is possible to identify this head in the phrase structure grammar, either using a reliable heuristic or due to annotation that marks the head of the phrase. When converting the

[2] Linguistic frameworks are independent of encoding systems, e.g., Penn Treebank's inline LISP-ish notation, can be converted to inline XML, offset annotation, etc., Such encoding differences are outside the scope of this report

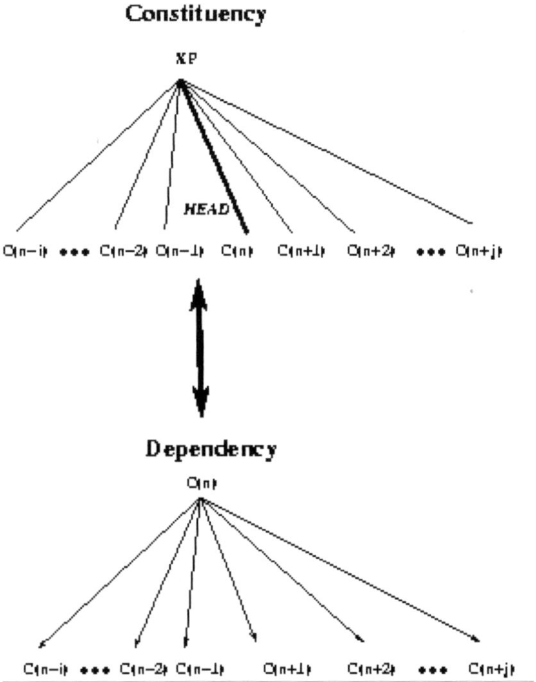

Fig. 1: Candidate Consituency/Dependency Mapping

phrase structure tree to the dependency tree, the rule promotes the head to the root of the tree. When converting a dependency tree to a phrase structure tree, the rule demotes the root to a constituent, possibly marking it as the head, and names the phrase based on the head's part of speech, e.g., nouns are heads of NPs. This rule is insufficient because: (1) Identifying the head of a phrase by heuristics is not 100% reliable and most phrase structure annotation does not include a marking for the head; (2) Some phrase structure distinctions do not translate well to some Dependency Grammars, e.g., the VP analysis and nestings of prenominal modifiers[3]; and (3) The rule only works for phrases that fit the head plus modifiers pattern and many phrases do not fit this pattern (uncontroversially).

While most assume that verbs act like the head of the sentence, a Subject + VP analysis of a sentence complicates this slightly. Regarding S-bars (relative clauses, that-S, subordinate-conjunction + S, etc.), there is some variation among theories whether the verb or the pre-S element (that, subordinate conjunction, etc.) is assigned the *head* label. Names, Dates, and other "patterned" phrases don't seem to have a unique head. Rather there are sets of constituents which together act like the head. For example, in *Dr. Mary Smith*, the string *Mary Smith* acts like the head. Idioms are big can of worms. Their headedness properties vary quite a bit. Sometimes they act like normal headed phrases and sometimes they don't. For example, the *phrase pull strings for John* obeys all the rules of English that would be expected of a verb phrase that consists of a verb, an NP and a complement PP. In contrast, the phrase *let alone* (Fillmore, et. al. 1988) has a syntax unique to that phrase. Semi-idiomatic constructions (including phrasal verbs, complex prepositions, etc.) raise some of the same questions as idioms. While making headedness assumptions similar to other phrases is relatively harmless, there is some variation. For example, in the phrase *Mary called Fred up on the phone*, there are two common views: (a) *called* is the head of the VP (or S) and *up* is a particle that depends on *called*; and (b) the VP has a complex head *called up*. For most purposes, the choice between these two analyses is arbitrary. Coordinate structures also require different treatment from head + modifier phrases -- there are multiple head-like constituents.

A crucial factor is that the notion *head* is used to represent different things. (cf. Corbett, et. al. 1993, Meyers 1995). However, there are two dominant notions. The first we will call the *functor* (following Categorial Grammar). The functor is the glue that holds the phrase together -- the word that selects for the other words, determines word order, licenses the construction, etc. For example, coordinate conjunctions are functors because they link the constituents in their phrase together. The second head like notion we will call the *thematic head,* the word or words that determine the external selectional properties of the phrase and usually the phrasal category as well. For example, in the noun phrase *the book and the rock*, the conjunction *and* is the functor, but the nouns and *book* and *rock* are thematic heads. The phrase is a concrete noun phrase due to *book* and *rock.* Thus the following sentence is well-formed: *I held the book and the rock*, but the following sentence is ill-formed **I held the noise and the redness.* Furthermore, the phrase *the book and the rock* is a noun phrase, not a conjunction phrase.

[3] The Prague Depedency Treebank orders dependency branches from the same head to represent the scope of the dependencies. Applicative Universal Grammar (Shauyman 1977) incorporates phrases into dependency structure.

In summary, there are some differences between phrase structure and dependency analyses which may be lost in translation, e.g., dependency analyses include head-marking by default and phrase structure analyses do not. On the other hand, phrase structure analyses include relations between groupings of words which may not always be preserved when translating to dependencies. Moreover, both identifying heads and combining words into phrases have their own sets of problems which can come to the forefront when translation between the two modalities is attempted. To be descriptively adequate, frameworks that mark heads do deal with these issues. The problem is that they are dealt with in different ways across dependency frameworks and across those phrase structure frameworks where heads are marked. For example, conjunction may be handled as being a distinct phenomenon (another dimension) that can be filtered through to the real heads. Alternatively, a head is selected on theoretical or heuristic grounds (the head of the first the conjunct, the conjunction, etc.) When working with multiple frameworks, a user must adjust for the assumptions of each framework.

3.2 Gap Filling Mechanisms

It is well-known that there are several equivalent ways to represent long distance and lexically based dependencies, e.g., (Sag and Fodor, 1994). Re-entrant graphs (graphs with shared structure), empty category/antecedent pairs, representations of discontinuous constituents, among other mechanisms can all be used to represent that there is some relation **R** between two (or more) elements in a linguistic structure that is, in some sense, noncanonical. The link by any of these mechanisms can be used to show that the relation **R** holds in spite of violations of a proximity constraint (long distance dependencies), a special construction such as control, or many other conditions. Some examples follow:

1. *What*$_i$ *did you read* e_i? *(WH extraction)*
2. *The terrorist*$_i$ was captured e_i *(Passive)*
3. *I*$_i$ *wanted* e_i *to accept it. (Control)*

It seems to us that the same types of cases are difficult for all such approaches. In the unproblematic cases, there is a gap (or equivalent) with a unique filler found in the same sentence. In the "difficult" cases, this does not hold. In some examples, the filler is hypothetical and should be interpreted something like the pronoun *anyone* (4 below) or the person being addressed (5). In other examples, the identity between filler and gap is not so straight-forward. In examples like (6), filler and gap are type identical, not token identical (they represent different *reading* events). In examples like (7), a gap can take split antecedents. Conventional filler/gap mechanims of all types have to be modified to handle these types of examples.

4. *They explained how e to drive the car*
5. e *don't talk to me*!
6. *Sally [read a linguistics article]*$_i$, *but John didn't* e_i.
7. *Sally*$_i$ *spoke with John*$_j$ *about e,,i,j,, leaving together.*

3.3 Coreference and Anaphora

There is little agreement concerning coreference annotation in the research community. Funding for the creation of the existing anaphorically annotated corpora (MUC6/7, ACE) has come primarily from initiatives focused on specific application tasks, resulting in task-oriented annotation schemes. On the other hand, a few (typically smaller) corpora have also been created to be consistent with existing, highly developed theoretical accounts of anaphora from a linguistic perspective. Accordingly, many schemes for annotating coreference or anaphora have been proposed, differing significantly with respect to: (1) the task definition, i.e., what type of semantic relations are annotated; (2) the flexibility that annotators have.

By far the best known and most used scheme is that originally proposed for MUC 6 and later adapted for ACE. This scheme was developed to support information extraction and its primary aim is to identify all mentions of the same objects in the text ('coreference') so as to collect all predications about them. A <coref> element is used to identify mentions of objects (the MARKABLES); each markable is given an index; subsequent mentions of already introduced objects are indicated by means of the REF attribute, which specifies the index of the previous mention of the same object. For example, in (1), markable 10 is a mention of the same object as markable 9. (This example is adapted from a presentation by Jutta Jaeger.)

1. <coref id="9">The New Orleans Oil and Gas [...] company</coref> added that <coref id="10" type="ident" ref="9"> it</coref> doesn't expect [...].

The purpose of the annotation is to support information extraction. To increase coding reliability, the MUC scheme conflates different semantic relations into a single IDENT relation. For example, coders marked pairs of NPs as standing in IDENT relations, even when these NPs would more normally be assumed to be in a predication relations, e.g., appositions as in 2 and NPs across a copula as in 3. This conflation of semantic relations is a convenient simplification in many cases but it is untenable in general, as discussed by van Deemter & Kibble (2001).

2. *Michael H. Jordan, the former head of Pepsico's international operations*
3. *Michael H. Jordan is the former head of Pepsico's international operations*

From the point of view of markup technology, the way used to represent coreference relations in MUC is very restrictive. Only one type of link can be annotated at a time: i.e., it is not possibly to identify a markable as being both a mention of a previously introduced referent and as a bridging reference on a second referent. In addition, the annotators do not have the option to mark anaphoric expressions as ambiguous.

The MATE `meta-scheme' (Poesio, 1999) was proposed as a very general repertoire of markup elements that could be used to implement a variety of existing coreference schemes, such as MUC or the MapTask scheme, but also more linguistically motivated schemes. From the point of view of markup technology, the two crucial differences from the MUC markup method are that the MATE meta-scheme is (i) based on standoff technology, and, most relevant for what follows, (ii) follows the recommendations of the Text Encoding Initiative (TEI) which suggest separating relations ('LINKs') from markables. LINKs can be used to annotate any form of semantic relations (indeed, the same notion was used in the TimeML annotation of temporal relations). A *structured* link, an innovation of MATE, can represent ambiguity (Poesio & Artstein, 2005). In (4), for example, the antecedent of the pronoun realized by markable ne03 in utterance 3.3 could be either *engine E2* or *the boxcar at Elmira*; with the MATE scheme, coders can mark their uncertainty.

4. *[in file markable.xml]*

3.3: hook <COREF:DE ID="ne01">*engine E2*</COREF:DE> to <COREF:DE ID="ne02"> *the boxcar at ... Elmira* </COREF:DE>

5.1: and send <COREF:DE ID="ne03"> *it*</COREF:DE> to <COREF:DE ID="ne04"> *Corning*</COREF:DE>

[in a separate file – e.g., link.xml]

<COREF:LINK HREF= "markable.xml#id(ne03)" type="ident">
<COREF:ANCHOR HREF= "markable.xml#id(ne01)" />
<COREF:ANCHOR HREF= "markable.xml#id(ne02)" />
</COREF:LINK>

The MATE meta-scheme also allowed a richer set of semantic relations in addition to IDENT, including PART-OF, PRED for predicates, etc., as well as methods for marking antecedents not explicitly introduced via an NP, such as plans and propositions. Of course, using this added power is only sensible when accompanied by experimentally tested coding schemes.

The MATE meta-scheme was the starting point for the coding scheme used in the GNOME project (Poesio 2004). In this project, a scheme was developed to model anaphoric relations in text in the linguistic sense—e.g., the information about discourse entities and their semantic relations expressed by the text. A relation called IDENT was included, but it was only used to mark the relation between mentions of the same discourse entity; so, for example, neither of the relations in (2) would be marked in this way.

From the point of view of coding schemes used for resource creation, the MATE meta-scheme gave rise to two developments: the standoff representation used in the MMAX annotation tool, and the Reference Annotation Framework (Salmon-Alt & Romary, 2004). MMAX was the first usable annotation tool for standoff annotation of coreference (there are now at least three alternatives: Penn's WordFreak, MITRE's CALISTO, and the NITE XML tools). The markup scheme was a simplification of the MATE scheme, in several respects. First of all, cross-level reference is not done using href links, but by specifying once and for all which files contain the base level and which files contain each level of representation; each level points to the same base level. Secondly, markables and coref links are contained in the same file.

5. [markable file]

```
<?xml version="1.0"?> <markables> ......
<markable id="markable_36" span=
"word_5,word_6, word_7“member="set_22" >
</markable> .... <markable id="markable_37"
span="word_14, word_15, word_16"
member="set_22" > </markable> ....
</markables>
```

The original version of MMAX, 0.94, only allowed to specify one identity link and one bridging reference per markable, but beginning version 2.0, multiple pointers are possible. An interesting aspect of the proposal is that identity links are represented by specifying membership to coreference chains instead of linking to previous mentions. Multiple pointers were used in the ARRAU project to represent ambiguous links, with some restrictions. The RAF framework was proposed not to directly support annotation, but as a rich enough markup framework to be used for annotation exchange.

3.3.2 Conversion

Several types of conversion between formats for representing coreference information are routinely performed. Perhaps the most common problem is to convert between inline formats used for different corpora: e.g., to convert the MUC6 corpus into GNOME. However, it is becoming more and more necessary to to convert standoff into inline formats for processing (e.g., MMAX into MAS-XML), and viceversa.

The increasing adoption of XML as a standard has made the technical aspect of conversion relatively straightforward, provided that the same information can be encoded. For example, because the GNOME format is richer than both the MUC and MMAX format, it should be straightforward to convert a MUC link into a GNOME link. However, the correctness of the conversion can only be ensured if the same coding instructions were followed; the MUC IDENT links used in (2) and (3) would not be expressed in the GNOME format as IDENT links. There is no standard method we know of for identifying these problematic links, although syntactic information can sometimes help. The opposite of course is not true; there is no direct way of representing the information in (4) in the MUC format. Conversion between the MAS-XML and the MMAX format is also possible, provided that pointers are used to represent both bridging references and identity links.

4 Predicate-Argument Relations

Predicate argument relations are labeled relations between two words/phrases of a linguistic description such that one is a semantic predicate or functor and the other is an argument of this predicate. In the sentence *The eminent linguist read the book,* there is a SUBJECT (or AGENT, READER, ARG0, DEPENDENT etc.) relation between the functor *read* and the phrase *The eminent linguist* or possibly the word *linguist* if assuming a dependency framework. Typically, the functor imposes selectional restrictions on the argument. The functor may impose word order restrictions as well, although this would only effect "local" arguments (e.g., not arguments related by WH extraction). Another popular way of expressing this relation is to say that *read* assigns the SUBJECT role to *The eminent linguist* in that sentence. Unfortunately, this way of stating the relation sometimes gives the false impression that a particular phrase can only be a member of one such relation. However, this is clearly not the case, e.g., in *The eminent linguist who John admires read the book*, *The eminent linguist* is the argument of: (1) a SUBJECT relation with *read* and an OBJECT relation with *admires*. Predicate-argument roles label relations between items and are not simply tags on phrases (like Named Entity Tags, for example).

There are several reasons why predicate argument relations are of interest for natural language processing, but perhaps the most basic reason is that they provide a way to factor out the common meanings from equivalent or nearly equivalent utterances. For example, most systems would represent the relation between *Mary* and *eat* in much the same way in the sentences: *Mary ate the sandwich*, *The sandwich was eaten by Mary*, and *Mary wanted to eat the sandwich*. Crucially, the shared aspect of meaning can be modeled as a relation with *eat* (or *ate*) as the functor and *Mary* as the argument (e.g., SUBJECT). Thus providing predicate argument relations can provide a way to generalize over data and, perhaps, allow systems to mitigate against the sparse data problem.

Systems for representing predicate argument relations vary drastically in granularity, In particular, there is a long history of disagreement about the appropriate level of granularity of role labeling, the tags used to distinguish between predicate argument relations. At one extreme, no distinction is made between predicate relations, one simply marks that the functor and argument are in a predicate-argument relation (e.g., unlabeled dependency trees). In another approach, one might distinguish among the arguments of each predicate with a small set of labels, sometimes numbered -- examples of this approach include Relational Grammar (Perlmutter 1984), PropBank and NomBank. These labels have different meanings for each functor, e.g., the subject of *eat*, *write* and *devour* are distinct. This assumes a very high level of granularity, i.e., there are several times the number of possible relations as there are distinct functors. So 1000 verbs may license as many as 5000 distinct relations. Under other approaches, a small set of relation types are generalized across functors. For example, under Relational Grammar's Universal Alignment Hypothesis (Perlmutter and Postal 1984, Rosen 1984), subject, object and indirect object relations are assumed to be of the same types regardless of verb. These terms thus are fairly coarse-grained distinctions between types of predicate/argument relations between verbs and their arguments.

Some predicate-neutral relations are more fine grained, including Panini's Karaka of 2000 years ago, and many of the more recent systems which make distinctions such as agent, patient, theme, recipient, etc. (Gruber 1965, Fillmore 1968, Jackendoff 1972). The (current) International Annotation of Multilingual Text Corpora project (http://aitc.aitc.net.org/nsf/iamtc/) takes this approach. Critics claim that it can be difficult to maintain consistency across predicates with these systems without constantly increasing the inventory of role labels to describe idiosyncratic relations, e.g., the relation between the verbs *multiply, conjugate*, and their objects. For example, only a very idiosyncratic classification could capture the fact that only a large round object (like the Earth) can be the object of *circumnavigate.* It can also be unclear which of two role labels apply. For example, there can be a thin line between a recipient and a goal, e.g., the prepositional object of *John sent a letter to the Hospital* could take one role or the other depending on a fairly subtle ambiguity.

To avoid these problems, some annotation research (and some linguistic theories) has abandoned predicate-neutral approaches, in favor of the approaches that define predicate relations on a predicate by predicate basis. Furthermore, various balances have been attempted to solve some of the problems of the predicate-neutral relations. FrameNet defines roles on a scenario by scenario basis, which limits the growth of the inventory of relation labels and insures consistency within semantic domains or frames. On the other hand, the predicate-by-predicate approach is arguably less informative then the predicate-neutral approach, allowing for no generalization of roles across predicates. Thus although PropBank/NomBank use a strictly predicate by predicate approach, there have been some attempts to regularize the numbering for semantically related predicates. Furthermore, the descriptors used by the annotators to define roles can sometimes be used to help make finer distinctions (descriptors often include familiar role labels like agent, patient, etc.)

The diversity of predicate argument labeling systems and the large inventory of possible role labels make it difficult to provide a simple mapping (like Table 1 for part of speech conversion) between these types of systems. The SemLink project provides some insight into how this mapping problem can be solved.

4.2 SemLink

SemLink is a project to link the lexical resources of FrameNet, PropBank, and VerbNet. The goal is to develop computationally explicit connections between these resources combining individual advantages and overcoming their limitations.

4.2.1 Background

VerbNet consists of hierarchies of verb classes, extended from those of Levin 1993. Each class and subclass is characterized extensionally by its set of verbs, and intensionally by argument lists and syntactic/semantic features of verbs. The full argument list consists of 23 thematic roles, and possible selectional restrictions on the arguments are expressed using binary predicates. VerbNet has been extended from the Levin classes, and now covers 4526 senses for 3175 lexemes. A primary emphasis for VerbNet is grouping verbs into classes with coherent syntactic and semantic characterizations in order to facilitate acquisition of new class members based on observable syntactic/semantic behavior. The hierarchical structure and small number of thematic roles is intended to support generalizations.

FrameNet consists of collections of semantic frames, lexical units that evoke these frames, and annotation reports that demonstrate uses of lexical units. Each semantic frame specifies a set of frame elements. These are elements that describe the situational props, participants and components that conceptually make up part of the frame. Lexical units appear in a variety of parts of speech, though we focus on verbs here. A lexical unit is a lexeme in a particular sense defined in its containing semantic frame. They are described in reports that list the syntactic realizations of the frame elements, and valence patterns that describe possible syntactic linking patterns. 3486 verb lexical units have been described in FrameNet which places a primary emphasis on providing rich, idiosyncratic descriptions of semantic properties of lexical units in context, and making explicit subtle differences in meaning. As such it could provide an important foundation for reasoning about context dependent semantic representations. However, the large number of frame elements and the current sparseness of annotations for each one has hindered machine learning.

PropBank is an annotation of 1M words of the Wall Street Journal portion of the Penn Treebank II with semantic role labels for each verb argument. Although the semantic roles labels are purposely chosen to be quite generic, i.e., Arg0, Arg1, etc., they are still intended to consistently annotate the same semantic role across syntactic variations, e.g., Arg1 in "John broke the window" is the same window (syntactic object) that is annotated as the Arg1 in "The window broke" (syntactic subject). The primary goal of PropBank is to provide consistent general labeling of semantic roles for a large quantity of text that can provide training data for supervised machine learning algorithms. PropBank can also provide frequency counts for (statistical) analysis or generation. PropBank includes a lexicon which lists, for each broad meaning of each annotated verb, its "frameset", the possible arguments, their labels and all possible syntactic realizations. This lexical resource is used as a set of verb-specific guidelines by the annotators, and can be seen as quite similar in nature to FrameNet, although much more coarse-grained and general purpose in the specifics.

To summarize, PropBank and FrameNet both annotate the same verb arguments, but assign different labels. PropBank has a small number of vague, general purpose labels with sufficient amounts of training data geared specifically to support successful machine learning. FrameNet provides a much richer and more explicit semantics, but without sufficient amounts of training data for the hundreds of individual frame elements. An ideal environment would allow us to train generic semantic role labelers on PropBank, run them on new data, and then be able to map the resulting PropBank argument labels on rich FrameNet frame elements.

The goal of SemLink is to create just such an environment. VerbNet provides a level of representation that is still tied to syntax, in the way that PropBank is, but provides a somewhat more fine-grained set of role labels and a set of fairly high level, general purpose semantic predicates, such as contact(x,y), change-of-location(x, path), cause(A, X), etc. As such it can be seen as a mediator between PropBank and FrameNet. In fact, our approach has been to use the explicit syntactic frames of VerbNet to semi-automatically map the PropBank instances onto specific VerbNet classes and role labels. The mapping can then be hand-corrected. In parallel, SemLink has been creating a mapping table from VerbNet class(es) to FrameNet frame(s), and from role label to frame element. This will allow the SemLink project to automatically generate FrameNet representations for every VerbNet version of a PropBank instance with an entry in the VerbNet-FrameNet mapping table.

4.2.2 VerbNet <==> FrameNet linking

One of the tasks for the SemLink project is to provide explicit mappings between VerbNet and FrameNet. The mappings between these two resources which have complementary information about verbs and disjoint coverage open several possibilities to increase their robustness. The fact that these two resources are now mapped gives researchers different levels of representation for events these verbs represent to be used in natural language applications. The mapping between VerbNet and FrameNet was done in two steps: (1) mapping VerbNet verb senses to FrameNet lexical units; (2) mapping VerbNet thematic roles to the equivalent (if present) FrameNet frame elements for the corresponding class/frame mappings uncovered during step 1.

In the first task, VerbNet verb senses were mapped to corresponding FrameNet senses, if available. Each verb member of a VerbNet class was assigned to a (set of) lexical units of FrameNet frames according to semantic meaning and to the roles this verb instance takes. These mappings are not one-to-one since VerbNet and FrameNet were built with distinctly different design philosophies. VerbNet verb classes are constructed by grouping verbs based mostly on their participation in diathesis alternations. In contrast, FrameNet is designed to group lexical items based on frame semantics, and a single FrameNet frame may contain sets of verbs with related senses but different subcategorization properties and sets of verbs with similar syntactic behavior may appear in multiple frames.

The second task consisted of mapping VerbNet thematic roles to FrameNet frame elements for the pairs of classes/frames found in the first task. As in the first task, the mapping is not always one-to-one as FrameNet tends to record much more fine-grained distinctions than VerbNet.

So far, 1892 VerbNet senses representing 209 classes were successfully mapped to FrameNet frames. This resulted in 582 VerbNet class – FrameNet frame mappings, across 263 unique FrameNet frames, for a total of 2170 mappings of VerbNet verbs to FrameNet lexical units.

4.2.3 PropBank <==> VerbNet linking

SemLink is also creating a mapping between VerbNet and PropBank, which will allow the use of the machine learning techniques that have been developed for PropBank annotations to generate more semantically abstract VerbNet representations. The mapping between VerbNet and PropBank can be divided into two parts: a "lexical mapping" and an "instance classifier."

The lexical mapping defines the set of possible mappings between the two lexicons, independent of context. In particular, for each item in the source lexicon, it specifies the possible corresponding items in the target lexicon; and for each of these mappings, specifies how the detailed fields of the source lexicon item (such as verb arguments) map to the detailed fields of the target lexicon item. The lexical mapping provides a set of possible mappings, but does not specify which of those mappings should be used for each instance; that is the job of the instance classifier, which looks at a source lexicon item in context, and chooses the most appropriate target lexicon items allowed by the lexical mapping.

The lexical mapping was created semi-automatically, based on an initial mapping which put VerbNet thematic roles in correspondence with individual PropBank framesets. This lexical mapping consists of a mapping between the PropBank framesets and VerbNet's verb classes; and a mapping between the roleset argument labels and the VerbNet thematic roles. During this initial mapping, the process of assigning a verb class to a frameset was performed manually while creating new PropBank frames. The thematic role assignment, on the other hand, was a semi-automatic process which finds the best match for the argument labels, based on their descriptors, to the set of thematic role labels of VerbNet. This process required human intervention due to the variety of descriptors for PropBank labels, the fact that the argument label numbers are not consistent across verbs, and gaps in frameset to verb class mappings.

To build the instance classifier, SemLink started with two heuristic classifiers. The first classifier works by running the SenseLearner WSD engine to find the WordNet class of each verb; and then using the existing WordNet/VerbNet mapping to choose the corresponding VerbNet class. This heuristic is limited by the performance of the WSD engine, and by the fact that the WordNet/VerbNet mapping is not available for all VerbNet verbs. The second heuristic classifier examines the syntactic context for each verb instance, and compares it to the syntactic frames of each VerbNet class. The VerbNet class with a syntactic frame that most closely matches the instance's context is assigned to the instance.

The SemLink group ran these two heuristic methods on the Treebank corpus and are hand-correcting the results in order to obtain a VerbNet-annotated version of the Treebank corpus. Since the Treebank corpus is also annotated with PropBank information, this will provide a parallel VerbNet/PropBank corpus, which can be used to train a supervised classifier to map from PropBank frames to VerbNet classes (and vice versa). The feature space for this machine learning classifier includes information about the lexical and syntactic context of the verb and its arguments, as well as the output of the two heuristic methods.

5. Version Control

Annotation compatibility is also an issue for related formalisms. Two columns in Table 1 are devoted to different CLAWS POS tagsets, but there are several more CLAWS tagsets (www.comp.lancs.ac.uk/ucrel/annotation.html), differing both in degree of detail and choice of distinctions made. Thus a detailed conversion table among even just the CLAWS tagsets may prove handy. Similar issues arise with the year to year changes of the ACE annotation guidelines (projects.ldc.upenn.edu/ace/) which include named entity, semantic classes for nouns, anaphora, relation and event annotation. As annotation formalisms mature, specifications can change to improve annotation consistency, speed or the usefulness for some specific task. In the interest of using old and new annotation together (more training data), it is helpful to have explicit mappings for related formalisms. Table 2 is a (preliminary) conversion table for Timex2 and Timex3, the latter of which can be viewed essentially as an elaboration of the former.

Table 3: Temporal Markup Translation Table[4]

Description	TIMEX2	TIMEX3	Comment
Contains a normalized form of the date/time	VAL="1964-10-16"	val="1964-10-16"	Some TIMEX2 points are TIMEX3 durations
Captures temporal modifiers	MOD="APPROX"	mod="approx"	---
Contains a normalized form of an anchoring data/time	ANCHOR_VAL ="1964-W22"	---	See TIMEX3 beginPoint and endPoint
Captures relative direction between VAL and ANCHOR_VAL	ANCHOR_DIR= "BEFORE"	---	See TIMEX3 beginPoint and endPoint
Identifies set expressions	SET="YES"	type="SET"	---
Provides unique ID number	ID="12"	tid="12"	Used to relate time expressions to other objects
Identifies type of expression	---	type="DATE"	Hold over from TIMEX. Derivable from format of VAL/val
Identifies indexical expressions	---	temporalFunction="true"	In TIMEX3, indexical expressions are normalized via a temporal function, applied as post-process
Identifies reference time used to compute val	---	anchorTimeID="t12"	Desired in TIMEX2
Identifies dis-	---	functionInDocu-	Used for date stamps on

[4] This preliminary table shows the attributes side by side with only one sample value, although other values are possible

course function		ment="CREATION_TIME"	documents
Captures anchors for durations	---	beginPoint="t11", end-Point="t12"	Captured by TIMEX2 AN-CHOR attributes
Captures quantification of a set expression	---	quant="EVERY"	Desired in TIMEX2
Captures number of reoccurences in set expressions	---	freq="2X"	Desired in TIMEX2

6. The Effect of Language Differences

Most researchers involved in linguistic annotation (particularly for NLP) take it for granted that coverage of a particular grammar for a particular language is of the utmost important. The (explanatory) adequacy of the particular linguistic theory assumed for multiple languages is considered a much less important. Given the diversity of annotation paradigms, we may go a step further and claim that it may be necessary to change theories when going from one language to another. In particular, language-specific phenomena can complicate theories in ways that prove unnecessary for languages lacking these phenomena. For example, English requires a much simpler morphological framework then languages like German, Russian, Turkish or Pashto. It has also been claimed on several occasions that a VP analysis is needed in some languages (English), but not others (Japanese). For the purposes of annotation, it would seem simplest to choose the simplest language-specific framework that is capable of capturing the distinctions that one is attempting to annotate. If the annotation is robust, it should be possible to convert it automatically into some language-neutral formalism should one arise that maximizes descriptive and explanatory adequacy. In the meanwhile, it would seem unnecessary to complicate grammars of specific languages to account for phenomena which do not occur in those languages.

6.1 The German TüBa-D/Z Treebank

German has a freer word order than English. This concerns the distribution of the finite verb and the distribution of arguments and adjuncts. German is a general Verb-Second language which means that in the default structure in declarative main clauses as well as in wh-questions the finite verb surfaces in second position preceded by only one constituent which is not necessarily the subject. In embedded clauses the finite verb normally occurs in a verb-phrase-final position following its arguments and adjuncts, and other non-finite verbal elements. German is traditionally assumed to have a head-final verb phrase. The ordering of arguments and adjuncts is relatively free. Firstly almost any constituent can be topicalised preceding the finite verb in Verb-Second position. Secondly the order of the remaining arguments and adjuncts is still relatively free. Ross (1967) coined the term Scrambling to describe the variety of linear orderings. Various factors are discussed to play a role here such as pronominal vs. phrasal constituency, information structure, definiteness and animacy (e.g. Uszkoreit 1986).

The annotation scheme of the German TüBa-D/Z treebank was developed with special regard to these properties of German clause structure. The main ordering principle is adopted from traditional descriptive analysis of German (e.g. Herling 1821, Höhle 1986). It partitions the clause into 'topological fields' which are defined by the distribution of the verbal elements. The top level of the syntactic tree is a flat structure of field categories including: Linke Klammer - left bracket (LK) and Rechte Klammer - verbal complex (VC) for verbal elements and Vorfeld - initial field (VF), C-Feld - complementiser field (C), Mittelfeld - middle field (MF), Nachfeld - final field (NF) for other elements.

Below the level of field nodes the annotation scheme provides hierarchical phrase structures except for verb phrases. There are no verb phrases annotated in TüBa-D/Z. It was one of the major design decisions to capture the distribution of verbal elements and their arguments and adjuncts in terms of topological fields instead of hierarchical verb phrase structures. The free word order would have required to make extensive use of traces or other mechanisms to relate dislocated constituents to their base positions, which in itself was problematic since there is no consensus among German linguists on what the base ordering is. An alternative which avoids commitment to specific base positions is to use crossing branches to deal with discontinuous constituents. This approach is adopted for example by the German TIGER treebank (Brants et al. 2004). A drawback of crossing branches is that the treebank cannot be modeled by a context free grammar. Since TüBa-D/Z was intended to be used for parser training, it was not a desirable option. Arguments and adjuncts are thus related to their predicates by means of functional labels. In contrast to the Penn Treebank, TüBa-D/Z assigns grammatical functions to all arguments and adjuncts. Due to the freer word order functions cannot be derived from relative positions only.

The choice of labels of grammatical functions is largely based on the insight that grammatical functions in German are directly related to the case assignment (Reis 1982). The labels therefore do not refer to grammatical functions such as subject, direct object or indirect object but make a distinction between complement and adjunct functions and classify the nominal complements according to their case marking: accusative object (OA), dative object (OD), genitive object (OG), and also nominative 'object' (ON) versus verbal modifier (V-MOD) or underspecified modifier (MOD).

Within phrases a head daughter is marked at each projection level. Exceptions are elliptical phrases, coordinate structures, strings of foreign language, proper names and appositions within noun phrases. Modifiers of arguments and adjuncts are assigned a default non-head function. In case of discontinuous constituents the function of the modifier is either explicitly marked by means of a complex label such as OA-MOD (the modifier of an accusative object) or by means of a secondary edge REFINT in case the modified phrase has a default head or non-head function itself (which holds in the case of e.g. NP complements of prepositions).

Figures 2 to 4 illustrate the German TüBa-D/Z treebank annotation scheme (Telljohann et al. (2005). – it combines a flat topological analysis with structural and functional information.

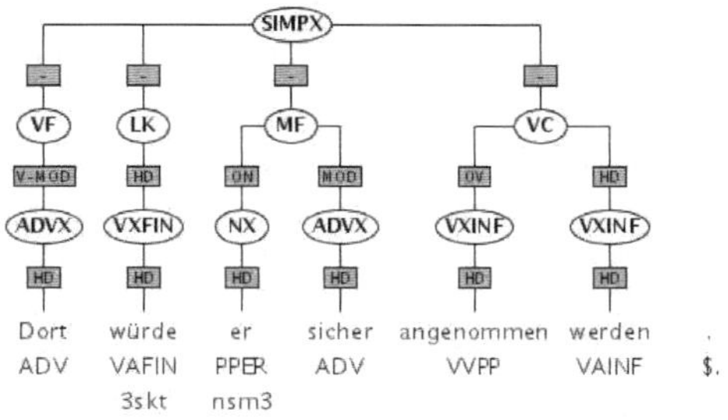

Fig. 2: verb-second
Dort würde er sicher angenommen werden.
there would he surely accepted be
'He would be surely accepted there.'

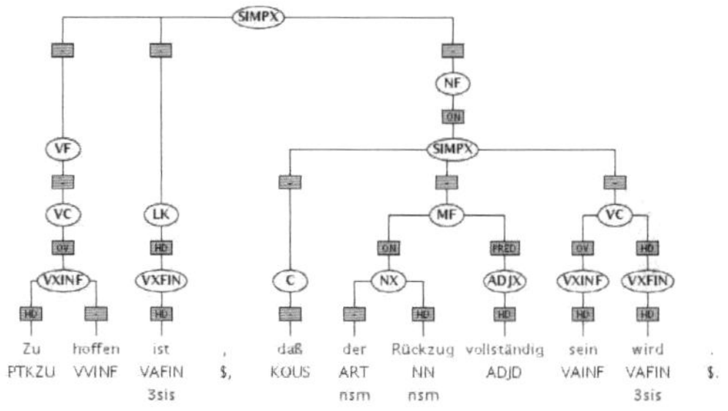

Fig. 3: verb-final
Zu hoffen ist, daß der Rückzug vollständig sein wird. to hope is that the fallback complete be will
'We hope that they will retreat completely.'

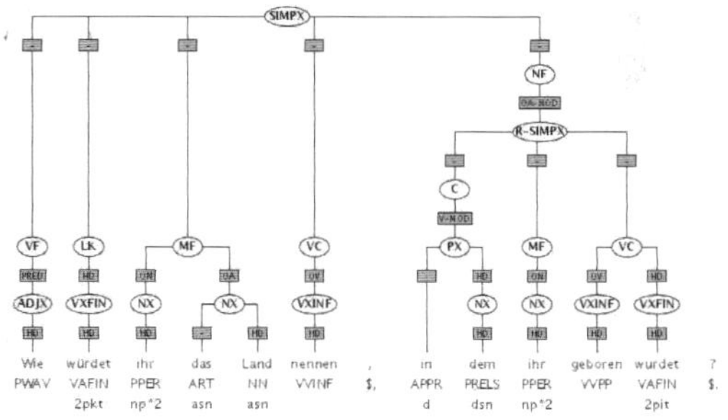

Fig. 4: discont. constituent marked OA-MOD
Wie würdet ihr das Land nennen, in dem ihr geboren wurdet?
how would you the country call in which you born were
'How would you call the country in which you were born?'

7. Concluding Remarks

This report has laid out several major annotation compatibility issues, focusing primarily on conversion among different annotation frameworks that represent the same type of information. We have provided procedures for conversion, along with their limitations. As more work needs to be done in this area, we intend to keep the online version available for cooperative elaboration and extension. Our hope is that the conversion tables will be extended and more annotation projects will incorporate details of their projects in order to facilitate compatibility.

The compatibility between annotation frameworks becomes a concern when (for example) a user attempts to use annotation created under two or more distinct frameworks for a single application. This is true regardless of whether the annotation is of the same type (the user wants more data for a particular phenomenon); or of different types (the user wants to combine different types of information).

Acknowledgement

This research was supported, in part, by the National Science Foundation under Grant CNI-0551615.

References

Brants, S., S. Dipper, P. Eisenberg, S. Hansen, E. Knig, W. Lezius, C. Rohrer, G. Smith & H. Uszkoreit, 2004. TIGER: Linguistic Interpretation of a German Corpus. In E. Hinrichs and K. Simov, eds, Research on Language and Computation, Special Issue. Volume 2: 597-620.

Chen, K.-J., Luo, C.-C., Gao, Z.-M., Chang, M.-C., Chen, F.-Y., and Chen, C.-J., 1999. The CKIP Chinese Treebank. In Journ ees ATALA sur les Corpus annot es pour la syntaxe, Talana, Paris VII: pp.85-96.

Chen, K.-J. et al. Building and Using Parsed Corpora, 2003. (A. Abeillé eds) KLUWER, Dordrecht. .

CKIP, 1995. Technical Report no. 95-02, the content and illustration of Sinica corpus of Academia Sinica. Inst. of Information Science.

G. Corbett, N. M. Fraser, and S. McGlashan, 1993. Heads in Grammatical Theory. Cambridge University Press, Cambridge.

K. Van Deemter and R. Kibble, 2001. On Coreferring: Coreference in MUC and related Annotation schemes. Journal of Computational Linguistics 26, 4, S. 629-637

C. Fillmore, 1968. The Case for Case. In E. Bach and R. T. Harms, eds, Universals in Linguistic Theory. Holt, Rinehart and Winston, NY

C. Fillmore, P. Kay & M. O'Connor. 1988. Regularity and Idiomaticity in Grammatical Constructions: The Case of *Let Alone*., Language, 64: 501-538.

J. S. Gruber, 1965. Studies in Lexical Relations. Ph.D. thesis, MIT

E. Hajicov and M. Ceplov, 2000. Deletions and Their Reconstruction in Tectogrammatical Syntactic Tagging of Very Large Corpora. In Proceedings of Coling 2000: pp. 278-284.

S. H. A. Herling, 1821. Über die Topik der deutschen Sprache. In Abhandlungen des frankfurterischen Gelehrtenvereins für deutsche Sprache. Frankfurt/M. Drittes Stück.

T. N. Höhle, 1986. Der Begriff `Mittelfeld'. Anmerkungen über die Theorie der topologischen Felder. In A. Schöne (Ed.), Kontroversen alte und neue. Akten des 7. Internationalen Germanistenkongresses Göttingen. 329-340.

R. Jackendoff, 1972. Semantic Interpretation in Generative Grammar. MIT Press, Cambridge.

P. Kingsbury and M. Palmer 2002. From treebank to propbank. In Proc. LREC-2002

H. Lee, C.-N. Huang, J. Gao and X. Fan, 2004. Chinese chunking with another type of spec. In SIGHAN-2004. Barcelona: pp. 41-48.

B. Levin 1993. English Verb Classes and Alternations: A Preliminary Investigation. Univ. of Chicago Press.

C. Manning and H. Schütze. 1999. Foundations of Statistical Natural Language Processing, MIT.

A. Meyers, R. Reeves, C. Macleod, R. Szekely, V. Zielinska, B. Young, and R. Grishman, 2004. The NomBank Project: An Interim Report. In NAACL/HLT 2004 Workshop Frontiers in Corpus Annotation.

A. Meyers, 1995. The NP Analysis of NP. In Papers from the 31st Regional Meeting of the Chicago Linguistic Society, pp. 329-342.

D. M. Perlmutter and P. M. Postal, 1984. The 1-Advancement Exclusiveness Law. In D. M. Perlmutter & C. G. Rosen, eds 1984. Studies in Relational Grammar 2. Univ. of Chicago Press.

D.. M. Perlmutter, 1984. Studies in Relational Grammar 1. Univ. of Chicago Press.

M. Poesio, 1999. Coreference, in MATE Deliverable 2.1, http://www.ims.uni-stuttgart.de/projekte/mate/mdag/cr/cr_1.html

M. Poesio, 2004. "The MATE/GNOME Scheme for Anaphoric Annotation, Revisited", Proc. of SIGDIAL.

M. Poesio and R. Artstein, 2005. The Reliability of Anaphoric Annotation, Reconsidered: Taking Ambiguity into Account. Proc. of ACL Workshop on Frontiers in Corpus Annotation.

J. Pustejovsky, A. Meyers, M. Palmer, and M. Poesio, 2005. Merging PropBank, NomBank, TimeBank, Penn Discourse Treebank and Coreference. In ACL 2005 Workshop: Frontiers in Corpus Annotation II: Pie in the Sky.

M. Reis, 1982. "Zum Subjektbegriff im Deutschen". In: Abraham, W. (Hrsg.): Satzglieder im Deutschen. Vorschläge zur syntaktischen, semantischen und pragmatischen Fundierung. Tübingen: Narr. 171-212.

C. G. Rosen, 1984. The Interface between Semantic Roles and Initial Grammatical Relations. In D.. M. Perlmutter and C. G. Rosen, eds, Studies in Relational Grammar 2. Univ. of Chicago Press.

J. R. Ross, 1967. Constraints on Variables in Syntax. Doctoral dissertation, MIT.

I. A. Sag and J. D. Fodor, 1994. Extraction without traces. In R. Aranovich, W. Byrne, S. Preuss, and M. Senturia, eds, Proc. of the Thirteenth West Coast Conference on Formal Linguistics, volume 13, CSLI Publications/SLA.

S. Salmon-Alt and L. Romary, RAF: towards a Reference Annotation Framework, LREC 2004

S. Shaumyan, 1977. Applicative Grammar as a Semantic Theory of Natural Language. Chicago Univ. Press.

H. Telljohann, E. Hinrichs, S. Kübler and H. Zinsmeister. 2005. Stylebook of the Tübinger Treebank of Written German (TüBa-D/Z). Technical report. University of Tübingen.

C. Thielen and A. Schiller, 1996. Ein kleines und erweitertes Tagset fürs Deutsche. In: Feldweg, H.; Hinrichs, E.W. (eds.): Wiederverwendbare Methoden und Ressourcen zur linguistischen Erschliessung des Deutschen. Vol. 73 of Lexicographica. Tübingen: Niemeyer. 193-203.

J.-L.Tsai, 2005. A Study of Applying BTM Model on the Chinese Chunk Bracketing. In LINC-2005, IJCNLP-2005, pp.21-30.

H. Uszkoreit, 1986. "Constraints on Order" in Linguistics 24.

F. Xia, M. Palmer, N. Xue, N., M. E. Okurowski, J. Kovarik, F.-D. Chiou, S. Huang, T. Kroch, and Marcus, M., 2000. Developing Guidelines and Ensuring Consistency for Chinese Text Annotation. In: Proc. of LREC-2000. Greece.

N. Xue, F. Chiou and M. Palmer. Building a Large-Scale Annotated Chinese Corpus, 2002. In: Proc. of COLING-2002. Taipei, Taiwan.

N. Xue, F. Xia, F.-D. Chiou and M. Palmer, 2005. The Penn Chinese TreeBank: Phrase Structure Annotation of a Large Corpus. Natural Language Engineering, 11(2)-207.

Manual Annotation of Opinion Categories in Meetings

Swapna Somasundaran[1], **Janyce Wiebe**[1], **Paul Hoffmann**[2], **Diane Litman**[1]
[1]Department of Computer Science, University of Pittsburgh, Pittsburgh, PA 15260
[2]Intelligent Systems Program, University of Pittsburgh, Pittsburgh, PA 15260
{swapna,wiebe,hoffmanp,litman}@cs.pitt.edu

Abstract

This paper applies the categories from an opinion annotation scheme developed for monologue text to the genre of multiparty meetings. We describe modifications to the coding guidelines that were required to extend the categories to the new type of data, and present the results of an inter-annotator agreement study. As researchers have found with other types of annotations in speech data, inter-annotator agreement is higher when the annotators both read and listen to the data than when they only read the transcripts. Previous work exploited prosodic clues to perform automatic detection of speaker emotion (Liscombe et al. 2003). Our findings suggest that doing so to recognize opinion categories would be a promising line of work.

1 Introduction

Subjectivity refers to aspects of language that express opinions, beliefs, evaluations and speculations (Wiebe et al. 2005). Many natural language processing applications could benefit from being able to distinguish between facts and opinions of various types, including speech-oriented applications such as meeting browsers, meeting summarizers, and speech-oriented question answering (QA) systems. Meeting browsers could find instances in meetings where opinions about key topics are expressed. Summarizers could include strong arguments for and against issues, to make the final outcome of the meeting more understandable. A preliminary user survey (Lisowska 2003) showed that users would like to be able to query meeting records with subjective questions like "Show me the conflicts of opinions between X and Y" , "Who made the highest number of positive/negative comments" and "Give me all the contributions of participant X in favor of alternative A regarding the issue I." A QA system with a component to recognize opinions would be able to help find answers to such questions.

Consider the following example from a meeting about an investment firm choosing which car to buy[1]. (In the examples, the words and phrases describing or expressing the opinion are underlined):

(1)[2] OCK: *Revenues of less than a million and losses of like five million <u>you know that's pathetic</u>*

Here, the speaker, OCK, shows his strong negative evaluation by using the expression "That's pathetic."

(2) OCK: *No it might <u>just be a piece of junk cheap piece of junk</u> that's <u>not a good investment</u>*

In (2), the speaker uses the term "just a piece of junk" to express his negative evaluation and uses this to argue for his belief that it is "not a good investment."

(3) OCK: *Yeah I think that's the <u>wrong image</u> for an investment bank he <u>wants stability and s safety</u> and you don't want <u>flashy like zip-</u>*

[1] Throughout this paper we take examples from a meeting where a group of people are deciding on a new car for an investment bank. The management wants to attract younger investors with a sporty car.

[2] We have presented the examples the way they were uttered by the speaker. Hence they may show many false starts and repetitions. Capitalization was added to improve readability.

Proceedings of the Workshop on Frontiers in Linguistically Annotated Corpora 2006, pages 54–61,
Sydney, July 2006. ©2006 Association for Computational Linguistics

ping around the corner kind of thing you know

The example above shows that the speaker has a negative judgment towards the suggestion of a sports car (that was made in the previous turn) which is indicated by the words "wrong image." The speaker then goes on to positively argue for what he wants. He further argues against the current suggestion by using more negative terms like "flashy" and "zipping around the corner." The speaker believes that "zipping around the corner" is bad as it would give a wrong impression of the bank to the customers. In the absence of such analyses, the decision making process and rationale behind the outcomes of meetings, which form an important part of the organization's memory, might remain unavailable.

In this paper, we perform annotation of a meeting corpus to lay the foundation for research on opinion detection in speech. We show how categories from an opinion (subjectivity) annotation scheme, which was developed for news articles, can be applied to the genre of multi-party meetings. The new genre poses challenges as it is significantly different from the text domain, where opinion analysis has traditionally been applied. Specifically, differences arise because:
1) There are many participants interacting with one another, each expressing his or her own opinion, and eliciting reactions in the process.
2) Social interactions may constrain how openly people express their opinions; i.e., they are often indirect in their negative evaluations.
We also explore the influence of speech on human perception of opinions.

Specifically, we annotated some meeting data with the opinion categories Sentiment and Arguing as defined in Wilson and Wiebe (2005). In our annotation we first distinguish whether a Sentiment or Arguing is being expressed. If one is, we then mark the polarity (i.e., positive or negative) and the intensity (i.e., how strong the opinion is). Annotating the individual opinion expressions is useful in this genre, because we see many utterances that have more than one type of opinion (e.g. (3) above). To investigate how opinions are expressed in speech, we divide our annotation into two tasks, one in which the annotator only reads the raw text, and the other in which the annotator reads the raw text and also listens to the speech. We measure inter-annotator agreement for both tasks.

We found that the opinion categories apply well to the multi-party meeting data, although there is some room for improvement: the Kappa values range from 0.32 to 0.69. As has been found for other types of annotations in speech, agreement is higher when the annotators both read and listen to the data than when they only read the transcripts. Interestingly, the advantages are more dramatic for some categories than others. And, in both conditions, agreement is higher for the positive than for the negative categories. We discuss possible reasons for these disparities.

Prosodic clues have been exploited to perform automatic detection of speaker emotion (Liscombe et al. 2003). Our findings suggest that doing so to recognize opinion categories is a promising line of work.

The rest of the paper is organized as follows: In Section 2 we discuss the data and the annotation scheme and present examples. We then present our inter-annotator agreement results in Section 3, and in Section 4 we discuss issues and observations. Related work is described in Section 5. Conclusions and Future Work are presented in Section 6.

2 Annotation

2.1 Data

The data is from the ISL meeting corpus (Burger et al. 2002). We chose task oriented meetings from the games/scenario and discussion genres, as we felt they would be closest to the applications for which the opinion analysis will be useful. The ISL speech is accompanied by rich transcriptions, which are tagged according to VERBMOBIL conventions. However, since real-time applications only have access to ASR output, we gave the annotators raw text, from which all VERBMOBIL tags, punctuation, and capitalizations were removed.

In order to see how annotations would be affected by the presence or absence of speech, we divided each raw text document into 2 segments. One part was annotated while reading the raw text only. For the annotation of the other part, speech as well as the raw text was provided.

2.2 Opinion Category Definitions

We base our annotation definitions on the scheme developed by Wiebe et al. (2005) for news articles. That scheme centers on the notion of subjectivity, the linguistic expression of private states. Private states are internal mental states that cannot be objectively observed or verified (Quirk et al. 1985) and include opinions, beliefs, judgments, evaluations, thoughts, and feelings. Amongst these many forms of subjectivity, we focus on the Sentiment and Arguing categories proposed by Wilson and Wiebe (2005). The categories are broken down by polarity and defined as follows:

Positive Sentiments: positive emotions, evaluations, judgments and stances.

(4) *TBC: Well ca How about one of the the newer Cadillac the Lexus is good*

In (4), taken from the discussion of which car to buy, the speaker uses the term "good" to express his positive evaluation of the Lexus .

Negative Sentiments: negative emotions, evaluations, judgments and stances.

(5) *OCK: I think these are all really bad choices*

In (5), the speaker expresses his negative evaluation of the choices for the company car. Note that "really" makes the evaluation more intense.

Positive Arguing: arguing for something, arguing that something is true or is so, arguing that something did happen or will happen, etc.

(6) *ZDN: Yeah definitely moon roof*

In (6), the speaker is arguing that whatever car they get should have a moon roof.

Negative Arguing: arguing against something, arguing that something is not true or is not so, arguing that something did not happen or will not happen, etc.

(7) *OCK: Like a Lexus or perhaps a Stretch Lexus something like that but that might be too a little too luxurious*

In the above example, the speaker is using the term "a little too luxurious" to argue against a Lexus for the car choice.

In an initial tagging experiment, we applied the above definitions, without modification, to some sample meeting data. The definitions covered much of the arguing and sentiment we observed. However, we felt that some cases of Arguing that are more prevalent in meeting than in news data needed to be highlighted more, namely Arguing opinions that are implicit or that underlie what is explicitly said. Thus we add the following to the arguing definitions.

Positive Arguing: expressing support for or backing the acceptance of an object, viewpoint, idea or stance by providing reasoning, justifications, judgment, evaluations or beliefs. This support or backing may be explicit or implicit.

(8) *MHJ: That's That's why I wanna What about the the child safety locks I think I think that would be a good thing because if our customers happen to have children*

Example (8) is marked as both Positive Arguing and Positive Sentiment. The more explicit one is the Positive Sentiment that the locks are good. The underlying Argument is that the company car they choose should have child safety locks.

Negative Arguing: expressing lack of support for or attacking the acceptance of an object, viewpoint, idea or stance by providing reasoning, justifications, judgment, evaluations or beliefs. This may be explicit or implicit.

(9) *OCK: Town Car But it's a little a It's a little like your grandf Yeah your grandfather would drive that*

Example (9) is explicitly stating who would drive a Town Car, while implicitly arguing against choosing the Town Car (as they want younger investors).

2.3 Annotation Guidelines

Due to genre differences, we also needed to modify the annotation guidelines. For each Arguing or Sentiment the annotator perceives, he or she identifies the words or phrases used to express it (the *text span*), and then creates an annotation consisting of the following.

- Opinion Category and Polarity
- Opinion Intensity
- Annotator Certainty

Opinion Category and Polarity: These are defined in the previous sub-section. Note that the *target* of an opinion is what the opinion is about. For example, the target of "John loves baseball" is baseball. An opinion may or may not have a separate target. For example, "want stability" in "We want stability" denotes a Positive Sentiment, and there is no separate target. In contrast, "good" in "The Lexus is good" expresses a Positive Sentiment and there is a separate target, namely the Lexus.

In addition to Sentiments toward a topic of discussion, we also mark Sentiments toward other team members (e.g. "Man you guys are so limited"). We do not mark agreements or disagreements as Sentiments, as these are different dialog acts (though they sometimes co-occur with Sentiments and Arguing).

Intensity: We use a slightly modified version of Craggs and Wood's (2004) emotion intensity annotation scheme. According to that scheme, there are 5 levels of intensity. Level "0" denotes a lack of the emotion (Sentiment or Arguing in our case), "1" denotes traces of emotion, "2" denotes a low level of emotion, "3" denotes a clear expression while "4" denotes a strong expression. Our intensity levels mean the same, but we do not mark intensity level 0 as this level implies the absence of opinion.

If a turn has multiple, separate expressions marked with the same opinion tag (category and polarity), and all expressions refer to the same target, then the annotators merge all the expressions into a larger text span, including the separating text in between the expressions. This resulting text span has the same opinion tag as its constituents, and it has an intensity that is greater than or equal to the highest intensity of the constituent expressions that were merged.

Annotator Certainty: The annotators use this tag if they are not sure that a given opinion is present, or if, given the context, there are multiple possible interpretations of the utterance and the annotator is not sure which interpretation is correct. This attribute is distinct from the Intensity attribute, because the Intensity attribute indicates the strength of the opinion, while the Annotator Certainty attribute indicates whether the annotator is sure about a given tag (whatever the intensity is).

2.4 Examples

We conclude this section with some examples of annotations from our corpus.

(10) *OCK: So Lexun had revenues of a hundred and fifty million last year and profits of like six million. That's pretty good*
Annotation: Text span=*That's pretty good* Category=Positive Sentiment Intensity=3 Annotator Certainty=Certain

The annotator marked the text span "That's pretty good" as Positive Sentiment because this this expression is used by OCK to show his favorable judgment towards the company revenues. The intensity is 3, as it is a clear expression of Sentiment.

(11) *OCK: No it might just be a piece of junk Cheap piece of junk that's not a good investment*
Annotation1: Text span=*it might just be a piece of junk Cheap piece of junk that's not a good investment* Category=Negative Sentiment Intensity=4 Annotator Certainty=Certain
Annotation2: Text span=*Cheap piece of junk that's not a good investment* Category =Negative Arguing Intensity=3 Annotator Certainty =Certain

In the above example, there are multiple expressions of opinions. In Annotation1, the expressions "it might just be a piece of junk", "cheap piece of junk" and "not a good investment" express negative evaluations towards the car choice (suggested by another participant in a previous turn). Each of these expressions is a clear case of Negative Sentiment (Intensity=3). As they are all of the same category and polarity and towards the same target, they have been merged by the annotator into one long expression of Intensity=4. In Annotation2, the sub-expression "cheap piece of junk that is not a good investment" is also used by the speaker OCK to argue against the car choice. Hence the annotator has marked this as Negative Arguing.

3 Guideline Development and Inter-Annotator Agreement

3.1 Annotator Training

Two annotators (both co-authors) underwent three rounds of tagging. After each round, discrepancies were discussed, and the guidelines were modified to reflect the resolved ambiguities. A total of 1266 utterances belonging to sections of four meetings (two of the discussion genre and two of the game genre) were used in this phase.

3.2 Agreement

The unit for which agreement was calculated was the turn. The ISL transcript provides demarcation of speaker turns along with the speaker ID. If an expression is marked in a turn, the turn is assigned the label of that expression. If there are multiple expressions marked within a turn with different category tags, the turn is assigned all those categories. This does not pose a problem for our evaluation, as we evaluate each category separately.

A previously unseen section of a meeting containing 639 utterances was selected and divided into 2 segments. One part of 319 utterances was annotated using raw text as the only signal, and the remaining 320 utterances were annotated using text and speech. Cohen's Kappa (1960) was used to calculate inter-annotator agreement. We calculated inter-annotator agreement for both conditions: raw-text-only and raw-text+speech. This was done for each of the categories: Positive Sentiment, Positive Arguing, Negative Sentiment, and Negative Arguing. To evaluate a category, we did the following:

- For each turn, if both annotators tagged the turn with the given category, or both did not tag the turn with the category, then it is a match.
- Otherwise it is a mismatch

Table 1 shows the inter-annotator Kappa values on the test set.

Agreement (Kappa)	Raw Text only	Raw Text + Speech
Positive Arguing	0.54	0.60
Negative Arguing	0.32	0.65
Positive Sentiment	0.57	0.69
Negative Sentiment	0.41	0.61

Table 1 Inter-annotator agreement on different categories.

With raw-text-only annotation, the Kappa value is in the moderate range according to Landis and Koch (1977), except for Negative Arguing for which it is 0.32. Positive Arguing and Positive Sentiment were more reliably detected than Negative Arguing and Negative Sentiment. We believe this is because participants were more comfortable with directly expressing their positive sentiments in front of other participants. Given only the raw text data, inter-annotator reliability measures for Negative Arguing and Negative Sentiment are the lowest. We believe this might be due to the fact that participants in social interactions are not very forthright with their Negative Sentiments and Arguing. Negative Sentiments and Arguing towards something may be expressed by saying that something else is better. For example, consider the following response of one participant to another participant's suggestion of aluminum wheels for the company car

(12) *ZDN: Yeah see what kind of wheels you know they have to look dignified to go with the car*

The above example was marked as Negative Arguing by one annotator (i.e., they should not get aluminum wheels) while the other annotator did not mark it at all. The implied Negative Arguing toward getting aluminum wheels can be inferred from the statement that the wheels should look dignified. However the annotators were not sure, as the participant chose to focus on what is desirable (i.e., dignified wheels). This utterance is actually both a general statement of what is desirable, and an implication that aluminum wheels are not dignified. But this may be difficult to ascertain with the raw text signal only.

When the annotators had speech to guide their judgments, the Kappa values go up significantly for each category. All the agreement numbers for raw text+speech are in the substantial range according to Landis and Koch (1977). We observe that with speech, Kappa for Negative Arguing has *doubled* over the Kappa obtained without speech. The Kappa for Negative Sentiment (text+speech) shows a 1.5 times improvement over the one with only raw text. Both these observations indicate that speech is able to help the annotators tag negativity more reliably. It is quite likely that a seemingly neutral sentence could sound negative, depending on the way words are stressed or pauses are inserted. Comparing the agreement on Positive Sentiment, we get a 1.2 times improvement by using speech. Similarly, agreement improves by 1.1 times for Positive Arguing when speech is used. The improvement with speech for the Positive categories is not as high as compared to negative categories, which conforms to our belief that people are more forthcoming about their positive judgments, evaluations, and beliefs.

In order to test if the turns where annotators were uncertain were the places that caused mismatch, we calculated the Kappa with the annotator-uncertain cases removed. The corresponding Kappa values are shown in Table 2

Agreement (Kappa)	Raw Text only	Raw Text + Speech
Positive Arguing	0.52	0.63
Negative Arguing	0.36	0.63
Positive Sentiment	0.60	0.73
Negative Sentiment	0.50	0.61

Table-2 Inter-annotator agreement on different categories, Annotator Uncertain cases removed.

The trends observed in Table 1 are seen in Table 2 as well, namely annotation reliability improving with speech. Comparing Tables 1 and 2, we see that for the raw text, the inter-annotator agreement goes up by 0.04 points for Negative Arguing and goes up by 0.09 points for Negative Sentiment. However, the agreement for Negative Arguing and Negative Sentiment on raw-text+ speech between Tables 1 and 2 remains almost the same. We believe this is because we had 20% fewer Annotator Uncertainty tags in the raw-text+speech annotation as compared to raw-text-only, thus indicating that some types of uncertainties seen in raw-text-only were resolved in the raw-text+speech due to the speech input. The remaining cases of Annotator Uncertainty could have been due to other factors, as discussed in the next section

Table 3 shows Kappa with the low intensity tags removed. The hypothesis was that low intensity might be borderline cases, and that removing these might increase inter-annotator reliability.

Agreement (Kappa)	Raw Text only	Raw Text + Speech
Positive Arguing	0.53	0.66
Negative Arguing	0.26	0.65
Positive Sentiment	0.65	0.74
Negative Sentiment	0.45	0.59

Table-3 Inter-annotator agreement on different categories, Intensity 1, 2 removed.

Comparing Tables 1 and 3 (the raw-text columns), we see that there is an improvement in the agreement on sentiment (both positive and negative) if the low intensity cases are removed. The agreement for Negative Sentiment (raw-text) goes up marginally by 0.04 points. Surprisingly, the agreement for Negative Arguing (raw-text) goes down by 0.06 points. Similarly in raw-text+speech results, removal of low intensity cases does not improve the agreement for Negative Arguing while hurting Negative Sentiment category (by 0.02 points). One possible explanation is that it may be equally difficult to detect Negative categories at both low and high intensities. Recall that in (12) it was difficult to detect if there is Negative Arguing at all. If the annotator decided that it is indeed a Negative Arguing, it is put at intensity level=3 (i.e., a clear case).

4 Discussion

There were a number of interesting subjectivity related phenomena in meetings that we observed during our annotation. These are issues that will need to be addressed for improving inter-annotator reliability.

Global and local context for arguing: In the context of a meeting, participants argue for (positively) or against (negatively) a topic. This may become ambiguous when the participant uses an explicit local Positive Arguing and an implicit global Negative Arguing. Consider the following speaker turn, at a point in the meeting when one participant has suggested that the company car should have a moon roof and another participant has opposed it, by saying that a moon roof would compromise the headroom.

(13) *OCK:* We <u>wanna make sure there's adequate headroom</u> for all those six foot six investors

In the above example, the speaker OCK, in the local context of the turn, is arguing positively that headroom is important. However, in the global context of the meeting, he is arguing against the idea of a moon roof that was suggested by a participant. Such cases occur when one object (or opinion) is endorsed which automatically precludes another, mutually exclusive object (or opinion).

Sarcasm/Humor: The meetings we analyzed had a large amount of sarcasm and humor. Issues arose with sarcasm due to our approach of marking opinions towards the content of the meeting (which forms the target of the opinion). Sarcasm is difficult to annotate because sarcasm can be

1) On topic: Here the target is the topic of discussion and hence sarcasm is used as a Negative Sentiment.

2) Off topic: Here the target is not a topic under discussion, and the aim is to purely elicit laughter.

3) Allied topic: In this case, the target is related to the topic in some way, and it's difficult to determine if the aim of the sarcasm/humor was to elicit laughter or to imply something negative towards the topic.

Multiple modalities: In addition to text and speech, gestures and visual diagrams play an important role in some types of meetings. In one meeting that we analyzed, participants were working together to figure out how to protect an egg when it is dropped from a long distance, given the materials they have. It was evident they were using some gestures to describe their ideas ("we can put tape like this") and that they drew diagrams to get points across. In the absence of visual input, annotators would need to guess what was happening. This might further hurt the inter-annotator reliability.

5 Related Work

Our opinion categories are from the subjectivity schemes described in Wiebe et al. (2005) and Wilson and Wiebe (2005). Wiebe et al. (2005) perform expression level annotation of opinions and subjectivity in text. They define their annotations as an *experiencer* having some type of *attitude* (such as Sentiment or Arguing), of a certain intensity, towards a target. Wilson and Wiebe (2005) extend this basic annotation scheme to include different types of subjectivity, including Positive Sentiment, Negative Sentiment, Positive Arguing, and Negative Arguing.

Speech was found to improve inter-annotator agreement in discourse segmentation of monologs (Hirschberg and Nakatani 1996). Acoustic clues have been successfully employed for the reliable detection of the speaker's emotions, including frustration, annoyance, anger, happiness, sadness, and boredom (Liscombe et al. 2003). Devillers et al. (2003) performed perceptual tests with and without speech in detecting the speaker's fear, anger, satisfaction and embarrassment. Though related, our work is not concerned with the speaker's emotions, but rather opinions toward the issues and topics addressed in the meeting.

Most annotation work in multiparty conversation has focused on exchange structures and discourse functional units like common grounding (Nakatani and Traum, 1998). In common grounding research, the focus is on whether the participants of the discourse are able to understand each other, and not their opinions towards the content of the discourse. Other tagging schemes like the one proposed by Flammia and Zue (1997) focus on information seeking and question answering exchanges where one participant is purely seeking information, while the other is providing it. The SWBD DAMSL (Jurafsky et al., 1997) annotation scheme over the Switchboard telephonic conversation corpus labels shallow discourse structures. The SWBD-DAMSL had a label "sv" for opinions. However, due to poor inter-annotator agreement, the authors discarded these annotations. The ICSI MRDA annotation scheme (Rajdip et al., 2003) adopts the SWBD DAMSL scheme, but does not distinguish between the opinionated and objective statements. The ISL meeting corpus (Burger and Sloane, 2004) is annotated with dialog acts and discourse moves like initiation and response, which in turn consist of dialog tags such as query, align, and statement. Their statement dialog category would not only include Sentiment and Arguing tags discussed in this paper, but it would also include objective statements and other types of subjectivity.

"Hot spots" in meetings closely relate to our work because they find sections in the meeting where participants are involved in debates or high arousal activity (Wrede and Shriberg 2003). While that work distinguishes between high arousal and low arousal, it does not distinguish between opinion or non-opinion or the different types of opinion. However, Janin et al. (2004) suggest that there is a relationship between dialog acts and involvement, and that involved utterances contain significantly more evaluative and subjective statements as well as extremely positive or negative answers. Thus we believe it may be beneficial for such works to make these distinctions.

Another closely related work that finds participants' positions regarding issues is argument diagramming (Rienks et al. 2005). This approach, based on the IBIS system (Kunz and Rittel 1970), divides a discourse into issues, and finds lines of deliberated arguments. However they do not distinguish between subjective and objective contributions towards the meeting.

6 Conclusions and Future Work

In this paper we performed an annotation study of opinions in meetings, and investigated the effects of speech. We have shown that it is possible to reliably detect opinions within multiparty conversations. Our consistently better agreement results with text+speech input over text-only input suggest that speech is a reliable indicator of opinions. We have also found that Annotator Uncertainty decreased with speech input. Our results also show that speech is a more informative indicator for negative versus positive categories. We hypothesize that this is due to the fact the people express their positive attitudes more explicitly. The speech signal is thus even more important for discerning negative opinions. This experience has also helped us gain insights to the ambiguities that arise due to sarcasm and humor.

Our promising results open many new avenues for research. It will be interesting to see how our categories relate to other discourse structures, both at the shallow level (agreement/disagreement) as well as at the deeper level (intentions/goals). It will also be interesting to investigate how other forms of subjectivity like speculation and intention are expressed in multiparty discourse. Finding prosodic correlates of speech as well as lexical clues that help in opinion detection would be useful in building subjectivity detection applications for multiparty meetings.

References

Susanne Burger and Zachary A Sloane. 2004. The ISL Meeting Corpus: Categorical Features of Communicative Group Interactions. *NIST Meeting Recognition Workshop 2004*, NIST 2004, Montreal, Canada, 2004-05-17

Susanne Burger, Victoria MacLaren and Hua Yu. 2002. The ISL Meeting Corpus: The Impact of Meeting Type on Speech Style. *ICSLP-2002*. Denver, CO: ISCA, 9 2002.

Jacob Cohen. 1960. A coefficient of agreement for nominal scales. *Educational and Psychological Meas.*, 20:37–46.

Richard Craggs and Mary McGee Wood. 2004. A categorical annotation scheme for emotion in the linguistic content of dialogue. *Affective Dialogue Systems.* 2004.

Laurence Devillers, Lori Lamel and Ioana Vasilescu. 2003. Emotion detection in task-oriented spoken dialogs. *IEEE International Conference on Multimedia and Expo (ICME).*

Rajdip Dhillon, Sonali Bhagat, Hannah Carvey and Elizabeth Shriberg. 2003. "Meeting Recorder Project: Dialog Act Labeling Guide," *ICSI Technical Report TR-04-002*, Version 3, October 2003

Giovanni Flammia and Victor Zue. 1997. Learning The Structure of Mixed Initiative Dialogues Using A Corpus of Annotated Conversations. *Eurospeech 1997*, Rhodes, Greece 1997, p1871—1874

Julia Hirschberg and Christine Nakatani. 1996. A Prosodic Analysis of Discourse Segments in Direction-Giving Monologues Annual Meeting- *Association For Computational Linguistics 1996*, VOL 34, pages 286-293

Adam Janin, Jeremy Ang, Sonali Bhagat, Rajdip Dhillon, Jane Edwards, Javier Mac´ıas-Guarasa, Nelson Morgan, Barbara Peskin, Elizabeth Shriberg, Andreas Stolcke, Chuck Wooters and Britta Wrede. 2004. "The ICSI Meeting Project: Resources and Research," *ICASSP-2004 Meeting Recognition Workshop*. Montreal; Canada: NIST, 5 2004

Daniel Jurafsky, Elizabeth Shriberg and Debra Biasca, 1997. *Switchboard-DAMSL Labeling Project Coder's Manual.* http://stripe.colorado.edu/˜jurafsky/manual.august1

Werner Kunz and Horst W. J. Rittel. 1970. Issues as elements of information systems. *Working Paper WP-131*, Univ. Stuttgart, Inst. Fuer Grundlagen der Planung, 1970

Richard Landis and Gary Koch. 1977. The Measurement of Observer Agreement for Categorical Data *Biometrics*, Vol. 33, No. 1 (Mar., 1977) , pp. 159-174

Agnes Lisowska. 2003. Multimodal interface design for the multimodal meeting domain: Preliminary indications from a query analysis study. *Technical Report IM2. Technical report, ISSCO/TIM/ETI.* Universit de Genve, Switserland, November 2003.

Jackson Liscombe, Jennifer Venditti and Julia Hirschberg. 2003. Classifying Subject Ratings of Emotional Speech Using Acoustic Features. *Eurospeech* 2003.

Christine Nakatani and David Traum. 1998. *Draft: Discourse Structure Coding Manual version 2/27/98*

Randolph Quirk, Sidney Greenbaum, Geoffry Leech and Jan Svartvik. 1985. *A Comprehensive Grammar of the English Language. Longman*, New York.s

Rutger Rienks, Dirk Heylen and Erik van der Weijden. 2005. Argument diagramming of meeting conversations. In Vinciarelli, A. and Odobez, J., editors, *Multimodal Multiparty Meeting Processing, Workshop at the 7th International Conference on Multimodal Interfaces*, pages 85–92, Trento, Italy

Janyce Wiebe, Theresa Wilson and Claire Cardie. 2005. Annotating expressions of opinions and emotions in language. *Language Resources and Evaluation (formerly Computers and the Humanities)*, volume 39, issue 2-3, pp. 165-210.

Theresa Wilson and Janyce Wiebe. 2005. Annotating attributions and private states. *ACL Workshop on Frontiers in Corpus Annotation II: Pie in the Sky.*

Britta Wrede and Elizabeth Shriberg. 2003. Spotting "Hotspots" in Meetings: Human Judgments and Prosodic Cues. *Eurospeech 2003*, Geneva

The Hinoki Sensebank
— A Large-Scale Word Sense Tagged Corpus of Japanese —

Takaaki Tanaka, Francis Bond and Sanae Fujita
{takaaki,bond,fujita}@cslab.kecl.ntt.co.jp
NTT Communication Science Laboratories,
Nippon Telegraph and Telephone Corporation

Abstract

Semantic information is important for precise word sense disambiguation system and the kind of semantic analysis used in sophisticated natural language processing such as machine translation, question answering, etc. There are at least two kinds of semantic information: lexical semantics for words and phrases and structural semantics for phrases and sentences.

We have built a Japanese corpus of over three million words with both lexical and structural semantic information. In this paper, we focus on our method of annotating the lexical semantics, that is building a word sense tagged corpus and its properties.

1 Introduction

While there has been considerable research on both structural annotation (such as the Penn Treebank (Taylor et al., 2003) or the Kyoto Corpus (Kurohashi and Nagao, 2003)) and semantic annotation (e.g. Senseval: Kilgariff and Rosenzweig, 2000; Shirai, 2002), there are almost no corpora that combine both. This makes it difficult to carry out research on the interaction between syntax and semantics.

Projects such as the Penn Propbank are adding structural semantics (i.e. predicate argument structure) to syntactically annotated corpora, but not lexical semantic information (i.e. word senses). Other corpora, such as the English Redwoods Corpus (Oepen et al., 2002), combine both syntactic and structural semantics in a monostratal representation, but still have no lexical semantics.

In this paper we discuss the (lexical) semantic annotation for the Hinoki Corpus, which is part of a larger project in psycho-linguistic and computational linguistics ultimately aimed at language understanding (Bond et al., 2004).

2 Corpus Design

In this section we describe the overall design of the corpus, and is constituent corpora. The basic aim is to combine structural semantic and lexical semantic markup in a single corpus. In order to make the first phase self contained, we started with dictionary definition and example sentences. We are currently adding other genre, to make the langauge description more general, starting with newspaper text.

2.1 Lexeed: A Japanese Basic Lexicon

We use word sense definitions from Lexeed: A Japanese Semantic Lexicon (Kasahara et al., 2004). It was built in a series of psycholinguistic experiments where words from two existing machine-readable dictionaries were presented to subjects and they were asked to rank them on a familiarity scale from one to seven, with seven being the most familiar (Amano and Kondo, 1999). Lexeed consists of all words with a familiarity greater than or equal to five. There are 28,000 words in all. Many words have multiple senses, there were 46,347 different senses. Definition sentences for these sentences were rewritten to use only the 28,000 familiar words. In the final configuration, 16,900 different words (60% of all possible words) were actually used in the definition sentences. An example entry for the word ドライバー *doraibā* "driver" is given in Figure 1, with English glosses added. This figure includes the sense annotation and information derived from it that is described in this paper.

Table 1 shows the relation between polysemy and familiarity. The #WS column indicates the average number of word senses that polysemous

Proceedings of the Workshop on Frontiers in Linguistically Annotated Corpora 2006, pages 62–69,
Sydney, July 2006. ©2006 Association for Computational Linguistics

INDEX		ドライバー *doraiba-*
POS		noun Lexical-Type `noun-lex`
FAMILIARITY		6.5 [1–7] (≥ 5) Frequency 37 Entropy 0.79
SENSE 1 (0.11)	DEFINITION	ねじ$_1$/を/差し入れ$_1$/たり/ 、/抜き取っ$_1$/たり/する/<u>道具$_1$</u>/。 a <u>tool</u> for inserting and removing screws .
	EXAMPLE	彼 は 細い ドライバー で 眼鏡 の ねじ を 締め た 。 he used a small screwdriver to tighten the screws on his glasses.
	HYPERNYM	道具$_1$ *equipment* "tool"
	SEM. CLASS	⟨`942:tool/implement`⟩ (⊂ ⟨`893:equipment`⟩)
	WORDNET	*screwdriver*$_1$
SENSE 2 (0.84)	DEFINITION	自動車$_1$/を/運転$_1$/する/<u>人$_1$</u>/。 <u>Someone</u> who drives a car.
	EXAMPLE	父 は 優良 な ドライバー として 表彰 さ れ た 。 my father was given an award as a good driver.
	HYPERNYM	人$_1$ *hito* "person"
	SEM. CLASS	⟨`292:chauffeur/driver`⟩ (⊂ ⟨`5:person`⟩)
	WORDNET	*driver*$_1$
SENSE 3 (0.05)	DEFINITION	ゴルフ$_1$/で/ 、/遠距離$_1$/用/の/クラブ$_3$/。一番/ウッド/。 In golf, a long-distance <u>club</u>. A number one wood.
	EXAMPLE	彼 は ドライバー で ３ ０ ０ ヤード 飛ばし た 。 he hit (it) 30 yards with the driver.
	HYPERNYM	クラブ$_3$ *kurabu* "club"
	SEM. CLASS	⟨`921:leisure equipment`⟩ (⊂ 921)
	WORDNET	*driver*$_5$
	DOMAIN	ゴルフ$_1$ *gorufu* "golf"

Figure 1: Entry for the Word *doraibā* "driver" (with English glosses)

words have. Lower familiarity words tend to have less ambiguity and 70 % of words with a familiarity of less than 5.5 are monosemous. Most polysemous words have only two or three senses as seen in Table 2.

Fam	#Words	Poly-semous	#WS	#Mono-semous(%)
6.5 -	368	182	4.0	186 (50.5)
6.0 -	4,445	1,902	3.4	2,543 (57.2)
5.5 -	9,814	3,502	2.7	6,312 (64.3)
5.0 -	11,430	3,457	2.5	7,973 (69.8)

Table 1: Familiarity vs Word Sense Ambiguity

#WS	#Words
1	18460
2	6212
3	2040
4	799
5	311
6	187
7	99
8	53
9	35
10	15
11	19
12	13
13	13
14	6
15	6
16	3
17	2
18	3
19	1
20	2
≥ 21	19

Table 2: Number of Word Senses

2.2 Ontology

We also have an ontology built from the parse results of definitions in Lexeed (Nichols and Bond, 2005). The ontology includes more than 50 thousand relationship between word senses, e.g. synonym, hypernym, abbreviation, etc.

2.3 Goi-Taikei

As part of the ontology verification, all nominal and most verbal word senses in Lexeed were linked to semantic classes in the Japanese thesaurus, Nihongo Goi-Taikei (Ikehara et al., 1997). Common nouns are classified into about 2,700 semantic classes which are organized into a semantic hierarchy.

2.4 Hinoki Treebank

Lexeed definition and example sentences are syntactically and semantically parsed with HPSG and correct results are manually selected (Tanaka et al., 2005). The grammatical coverage over all sentences is 86%. Around 12% of the parsed sentences were rejected by the treebankers due to an incomplete semantic representation. This process had been done independently of word sense annotation.

2.5 Target Corpora

We chose two types of corpus to mark up: a dictionary and two newspapers. Table 3 shows basic statistics of the target corpora.

The dictionary Lexeed, which defined word senses, is also used for a target for sense tagging. Its definition (LXD-DEF) and example (LXD-EX) sentences consist of basic words and function words only, i.e. it is self-contained. Therefore, all content words have headwords in Lexeed, and all word senses appear in at least one example sentence.

Both newspaper corpora where taken from the Mainichi Daily News. One sample (Senseval2) was the text used for the Japanese dictionary task in Senseval-2 (Shirai, 2002), which has some words marked up with word sense tags defined in the Iwanami lexicon (Nishio et al., 1994). The second sample was those sentences used in the Kyoto Corpus (Kyoto), which is marked up with dependency analyses (Kurohashi and Nagao, 2003). We chose these corpora so that we can compare our annotation with existing annotation. Both these corpora were thus already segmented and annotated with parts-of-speech. However, they used different morphological analyzers to the one used in Lexeed, so we had to do some remapping. E.g. in Kyoto the copula is not split from nominal-adjectives, whereas in Lexeed it is: 元気だ *genkida* "lively" vs 元気 だ *genki da*. This could be done automatically after we had written a few rules.

Although the newspapers contain many words other than basic words, only basic words have sense tags. Also, a word unit in the newspapers does not necessarily coincide with the headword in Lexeed since part-of-speech taggers used for annotation are different. We do not adjust the word segmentation and leave it untagged at this stage, even if it is a part of a basic word or consists of multiple basic words. For instance, Lexeed has the compound entry 貨幣価値 *kahei-kachi* "monetary value", however, this word is split into two basic words in the corpora. In this case, both two words 貨幣 *kahei* "money" and 価値 *kachi* "value" are tagged individually.

Corpus	Tokens	Content Words	Basic Words	%Mono-semous
LXD-DEF	691,072	318,181	318,181	31.7
LXD-EX	498,977	221,224	221,224	30.5
Senseval2	888,000	692,069	391,010	39.3
Kyoto	969,558	526,760	472,419	36.3

Table 3: Corpus Statistics

The corpora are not fully balanced, but allow some interesting comparisons. There are effectively three genres: dictionary definitions, which tend to be fragments and are often syntactically highly ambiguous; dictionary example sentences, which tend to be short complete sentences, and are easy to parse; and newspaper text from two different years.

3 Annotation

Each word was annotated by five annotators. We actually used 15 annotators, divided into 3 groups. None were professional linguists or lexicographers. All of them had a score above 60 on a Chinese character based vocabulary test (Amano and Kondo, 1998). We used multiple annotators to measure the confidence of tags and the degree of difficulty in identifying senses.

The target words for sense annotation are the 9,835 headwords having multiple senses in Lexeed (§ 2.1). They have 28,300 senses in all. Monosemous words were not annotated. Annotation was done word by word. Annotators are presented multiple sentences (up to 50) that contain the same target word, and they keep tagging that word until occurrences are done. This enables them to compare various contexts where a target word appears and helps them to keep the annotation consistent.

3.1 Tool

A screen shot of the annotation tool is given in Figure 2. The interface uses frames on a browser, with all information stored in SQL tables. The left hand frame lists the words being annotated. Each word is shown with some context: the surrounding paragraph, and the headword for definition and example sentences. These can be clicked on to get more context. The word being annotated is highlighted in red. For each word, the annotator chooses its senses or one or more of the other tags as clickable buttons. It is also possible to choose one tag as the default for all entries on the screen.

The right hand side frame has the dictionary definitions for the word being tagged in the top frame, and a lower frame with instructions. A single word may be annotated with senses from more than one headword. For example バス is divided into two headwords *basu* "bus" and *basu* "bass", both of which are presented.

As we used a tab-capable browser, it was easy for the annotators to call up more information in different tabs. This proved to be quite popular.

3.2 Markup

Annotators choose the most suitable sense in the given context from the senses that the word have in lexicon. Preferably, they select a single sense for a word, although they can mark up multiple tags if the words have multiple meanings or are truly ambiguous in the contexts.

When they cannot choose a sense in some reasons, they choose one or more of the following special tags.

- **o** *other sense*: an appropriate sense is not found in a lexicon. Relatively novel concepts (e.g. ドライバー *doraibā* "driver" for "software driver") are given this tag.
- **c** *multiword expressions (compound / idiom)*: the target word is a part of a non-compositional compound or idiom.
- **p** *proper noun*: the word is a proper noun.
- **x** *homonym*: an appropriate entry is not found in a lexicon, because a target is different from head words in a lexicon (e.g. only a headword バス *bass* "bus" is present in a lexicon for バス*basu* "bass").
- **e** *analysis error*: the word segmentation or part-of-speech is incorrect due to errors in pre-annotation of the corpus.

3.3 Feedback

One of the things that the annotators found hard was not knowing how well they were doing. As they were creating a gold standard, there was initially no way of knowing how correct they were. We also did not know at the start of the annotation how fast senses could or should be annotated (a test of the tool gave us an initial estimate of around 400 tokens/day).

To answer these questions, and to provide feedback for the annotators, twice a day we calculated and graphed the speed (in words/day) and majority agreement (how often an annotator agrees with the majority of annotators for each token, measured over all words annotated so far). Each annotator could see a graph with their results labelled, and the other annotators made anonymous. The results are grouped into three groups of five annotators. Each group is annotating a different set of words, but we included them all in the feedback. The order within each group is sorted by agreement, as we wished to emphasise the importance of agreement over speed. An example of a graph is given in Figure 3. When this feedback was given, this particular annotator has the second worst agreement score in their subgroup (90.27%) and is reasonably fast (1799 words/day) — they should slow down and think more.

The annotators welcomed this feedback, and complained when our script failed to produce it. There was an enormous variation in speed: the fastest annotator was 4 times as fast as the slowest, with no appreciable difference in agreement. After providing the feedback, the average speed increased considerably, as the slowest annotators agonized less over their decisions. The final average speed was around 1,500 tokens/day, with the fastest annotator still almost twice as fast as the slowest.

4 Inter-Annotator Agreement

We employ inter-annotator agreement as our core measure of annotation consistency, in the same way we did for treebank evaluation (Tanaka et al., 2005). This agreement is calculated as the average of pairwise agreement. Let w_i be a word in a set of content words W and $w_{i,j}$ be the jth occurrence of a word w_i. Average pairwise agreement between the sense tags of $w_{i,j}$ each pair of annotators marked up $a(w_{i,j})$ is:

$$a(w_{i,j}) = \frac{\sum_k \left({}_{m_{i,j}(s_{ik})}C_2\right)}{{}_{n_{w_{i,j}}}C_2} \quad (1)$$

where $n_{w_{i,j}} (\geq 2)$ is the number of annotators that tag the word $w_{i,j}$, and $m_{i,j}(s_{ik})$ is the number

Figure 2: Sense Annotation tool (word 暫く *shibaraku* “briefly”)

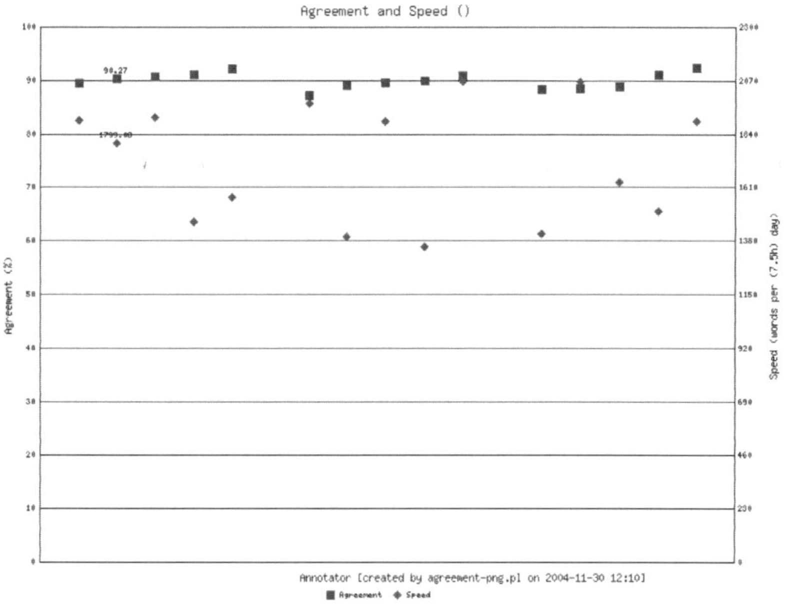

Figure 3: Sample feedback provided to an annotator

of sense tags s_{ik} for the word $w_{i,j}$. Hence, the agreement of the word w_i is the average of $a_{w_{i,j}}$ over all occurrences in a corpus:

$$a(w_i) = \frac{\sum_j a(w_{i,j})}{N_{w_i}} \tag{2}$$

where N_{w_i} is the frequency of the word w_i in a corpus.

Table 4 shows statistics about the annotation results. The average numbers of word senses in the newspapers are lower than the ones in the dictionary and, therefore, the token agreement of the newspapers is higher than those of the dictionary sentences. %Unanimous indicates the ratio of tokens vs types for which all annotators (normally five) choose the same sense. Snyder and Palmer (2004) report 62% of all word types on the English all-words task at SENSEVAL-3 were labelled unanimously. It is hard to directly compare with our task since their corpus has only 2,212 words tagged by two or three annotators.

4.1 Familiarity

As seen in Table 5, the agreement per type does not vary much by familiarity. This was an unexpected result. Even though the average polysemy is high, there are still many highly familiar words with very good agreement.

Fam	Agreement token (type)	#WS	%Monosem
6.5 -	.723 (.846)	7.00	22.6
6.0 -	.780 (.846)	5.82	28.0
5.5 -	.813 (.853)	3.79	42.4
5.0 -	.821 (.850)	3.84	46.2
ALL	.787 (.850)	5.18	34.5

Table 5: Inter-Annotator Agreement (LXD-DEF)

4.2 Part-of-Speech

Table 6 shows the agreement according to part of speech. Nouns and verbal nouns (vn) have the highest agreements, similar to the results for the English all-words task at SENSEVAL-3 (Snyder and Palmer, 2004). In contrast, adjectives have as low agreement as verbs, although the agreement of adjectives was the highest and that of verbs was the lowest in English. This partly reflects differences in the part of speech divisions between Japanese and English. Adjectives in Japanese are much close in behaviour to verbs (e.g. they can head sentences) and includes many words that are translated as verbs in English.

4.3 Entropy

Entropy is directly related to the difficulty in identifing senses as shown in Table 7.

POS	Agreement (type)	#WS	%Monosemous
n	.803 (.851)	2.86	62.9
v	.772 (.844)	3.65	34.0
vn	.849 (.865)	2.54	61.0
adj	.770 (.810)	3.58	48.3
adv	.648 (.833)	3.08	46.4
others	.615 (.789)	3.19	50.8

Table 6: POS vs Inter-Annotator Agreement (LXD-DEF)

Entropy	Agreement (type)	#Words	#WS
2 -	.672	84	14.2
1 -	.758	1096	4.38
0.5 -	.809	1627	2.88
0.05 -	.891	495	3.19
0 -	.890	13778	2.56

Table 7: Entropy vs Agreement

4.4 Sense Lumping

Low agreement words have some senses that are difficult to distinguish from each other: these senses often have the same hypernyms. For example, the agreement rate of 草花 *kusabana* "grass/flower" in LXD-DEF is only 33.7 %. It has three senses whose semantic class is similar: *kusabana*$_1$ "flower that blooms in grass", *kusabana*$_2$ "grass that has flowers" and *souka*$_1$ "grass and flowers" (hypernyms flower$_1$, grass$_1$ and flower$_1$ & grass$_1$ respectively).

In order to investigate the effect of semantic similarity on agreement, we lumped similar word senses based on hypernym and semantic class. We use hypernyms from the ontology (§ 2.1) and semantic classes in Goi-Taikei (§ 2.3), to regard the word senses that have the same hypernyms or belong to the same semantic classes as the same senses.

Table 8 shows the distribution after sense lumping. Table 9 shows the agreement with lumped senses. Note that this was done with an automatically derived ontology that has not been fully hand corrected.

As is expected, the overall agreement increased, from 0.787 to 0.829 using the ontology, and to 0.835 using the coarse-grained Goi-Taikei semantic classes. For many applications, we expect that this level of disambiguation is all that is required.

4.5 Special Tags

Table 10 shows the ratio of special tags and multiple tags to all tags. These results show

Corpus	Annotated Tokens	#WS	Agreement token (type)	%Unanimous token (type)	Kappa
LXD-DEF	199,268	5.18	.787 (.850)	62.8 (41.1)	0.58
LXD-EX	126,966	5.00	.820 (.871)	69.1 (53.2)	0.65
Senseval2	223,983	4.07	.832 (.833)	73.9 (45.8)	0.52
Kyoto	268,597	3.93	.833 (.828)	71.5 (46.1)	0.50

Table 4: Basic Annotation Statistics

Corpus	%Other Sense	%MWE	%Homonym	%Proper Noun	%Error	%Multiple Tags
LXD-DEF	4.2	1.5	0.084	0.046	0.92	11.9
LXD-EX	2.3	0.44	0.035	0.0018	0.43	11.6
Senseval2	9.3	5.6	4.1	8.7	5.7	7.9
Kyoto	9.8	7.9	3.3	9.0	5.5	9.3

Table 10: Special Tags and Multiple Tags

Fam	Agreement token (type)	#WS	%Monosem
6.5 -	.772 (.863)	6.37	25.6
6.0 -	.830 (.868)	5.16	31.5
5.5 -	.836 (.872)	3.50	45.6
5.0 -	.863 (.866)	3.76	58.7
ALL	.829 (.869)	4.72	39.1

Lumping together Hypernyms
(4,380 senses compressed into 1,900 senses)

Fam	Agreement token (type)	#WS	%Monosem
6.5 -	.775 (.890)	6.05	26.8
6.0 -	.835 (.891)	4.94	36.4
5.5 -	.855 (.894)	3.29	50.6
5.0 -	.852 (.888)	3.46	49.9
ALL	.835 (.891)	4.48	41.7

Lumping together Semantic Classes
(8,691 senses compressed into 4,030 senses)

Table 8: Sense Lumping Results (LXD-DEF)

(LXD-DEF)	Agreement token (type)	#WS	%Monosem
no lumping	.698 (.816)	8.81	0.0
lumping	.811 (.910)	8.24	20.0

Hypernum Lumping

(LXD-DEF)	Agreement token (type)	#WS	%Monosem
no lumping	.751 (.814)	7.09	0.0
lumping	.840 (.925)	5.99	21.9

Semantic Class Lumping

Table 9: Lumped Sense Agreement (LXD-DEF)

the differences in corpus characteristics between dictionary and newspaper. The higher ratios of Other Sense and Homonym at newspapers indicate that the words whose surface form is in a dictionary are frequently used for the different meanings in real text, e.g. 銀 *gin* "silver" is used for the abbrebiation of 銀行 *ginkou* "bank". %Multiple Tags is the percentage of tokens for which at least one annotator marked multiple tags.

5 Discussion

5.1 Comparison with Senseval-2 corpus

The Senseval-2 Japanese dictionary task annotation used senses from a different dictionary (Shirai, 2002). In the evaluation, 100 test words were selected from three groups with different entropy bands (Kurohashi and Shirai, 2001). D_a is the highest entropy group, which contains the most hard to tag words, and D_c is the lowest entropy group.

We compare our results with theirs in Table 11. The Senseval-2 agreement figures are slightly higher than our overall. However, it is impossible to make a direct comparison as the numbers of annotators (two or three annotators in Senseval vs more than 5 annotators in our work) and the sense inventories are different.

5.2 Problems

Two main problems came up when building the corpora: word segmentation and sense segmentation. Multiword expressions like compounds and idioms are tied closely to both problems.

The word segmentation is the problem of how to determine an unit expressing a meaning. At the present stage, it is based on headword in Lexeed, in particular, only compounds in Lexeed are recognized, we do not discriminate non-decomposable compounds with decomposable ones. However, if the headword unit in the dictionary is inconsistent, word sense tagging inherits this problem. For examples, 一部 *ichibu* has two main usage: one + classifier and a part of something. Lexeed has an entry including both two senses. However, the former is split into two

POS	D_a		D_b		D_c		Total	
	Hinoki	Senseval	Hinoki	Senseval	Hinoki	Senseval	Hinoki	Senseval
noun	.768	.809	.784	.786	.848	.957	.806	.859
	14.4	13.1	5.0	4.1	3.1	3.8	5.9	5.1
verb	.660	.699	.722	.896	.738	.867	.723	.867
	16.7	21.8	10.3	9.3	5.2	5.9	9.6	10.9
total	.710	.754	.760	.841	.831	.939	.768	.863
	15.6	18.8	7.0	6.2	4.2	4.9	7.6	7.9

Table 11: Comparison of Agreement for the Senseval-2 Lexical Sample Task Corpus (upper row: agreement, lower row: the number of word senses)

words by our morphological analyser in the same way as other numeral + classifier.

The second problem is how to mark off metaphorical meaning from literal meanings. Currently, this also depends on the Lexeed definition and it is not necessarily consistent either. Some words in institutional idioms (Sag et al., 2002) have the idiom sense in the lexicon while most words do not. For instance, 尻尾 *shippo* "tail of animal") has a sense for the reading "weak point" in an idiom 尻尾を掴む *shippo-o tsukamu* "lit. to grasp the tail, idiom. to find one's weak point", while 汗 *ase* "sweat" does not have a sense for the applicable meaning in the idiom 汗を流す *ase-o nagasu* "lit. to sweat, idiom, to work hard".

6 Conclusions

We built a corpus of over three million words which has lexical semantic information. We are currently using it to build a model for word sense disambiguation.

Acknowledgement

We thank the 15 sense annotators and 3 treebankers (Takayuki Kuribayashi, Tomoko Hirata and Koji Yamashita).

References

Anne Abeillé, editor. 2003. *Treebanks: Building and Using Parsed Corpora*. Kluwer Academic Publishers.

Shigeaki Amano and Tadahisa Kondo. 1998. Estimation of mental lexicon size with word familiarity database. In *International Conference on Spoken Language Processing*, volume 5, pages 2119–2122.

Shigeaki Amano and Tadahisa Kondo. 1999. *Nihongo-no Goi-Tokusei (Lexical properties of Japanese)*. Sanseido.

Francis Bond, Sanae Fujita, Chikara Hashimoto, Kaname Kasahara, Shigeko Nariyama, Eric Nichols, Akira Ohtani, Takaaki Tanaka, and Shigeaki Amano. 2004. The Hinoki treebank: A treebank for text understanding. In *Proceedings of the First International Joint Conference on Natural Language Processing (IJCNLP-04)*, pages 554–559. Hainan Island.

Satoru Ikehara, Masahiro Miyazaki, Satoshi Shirai, Akio Yokoo, Hiromi Nakaiwa, Kentaro Ogura, Yoshifumi Ooyama, and Yoshihiko Hayashi. 1997. *Goi-Taikei — A Japanese Lexicon*. Iwanami Shoten, Tokyo. 5 volumes/CDROM.

Kaname Kasahara, Hiroshi Sato, Francis Bond, Takaaki Tanaka, Sanae Fujita, Tomoko Kanasugi, and Shigeaki Amano. 2004. Construction of a Japanese semantic lexicon: Lexeed. SIG NLC-159, IPSJ, Tokyo. (in Japanese).

Adam Kilgariff and Joseph Rosenzweig. 2000. Framework and results for English SENSEVAL. *Computers and the Humanities*, 34(1–2):15–48. Special Issue on SENSEVAL.

Sadao Kurohashi and Makoto Nagao. 2003. Building a Japanese parsed corpus — while improving the parsing system. In Abeillé (2003), chapter 14, pages 249–260.

Sadao Kurohashi and Kiyoaki Shirai. 2001. SENSEVAL-2 Japanese task. SIG NLC 2001-10, IEICE. (in Japanese).

Eric Nichols and Francis Bond. 2005. Acquiring ontologies using deep and shallow processing. In *11th Annual Meeting of the Association for Natural Language Processing*, pages 494–498. Takamatsu.

Minoru Nishio, Etsutaro Iwabuchi, and Shizuo Mizutani. 1994. *Iwanami Kokugo Jiten Dai Go Han [Iwanami Japanese Dictionary Edition 5]*. Iwanami Shoten, Tokyo. (in Japanese).

Stephan Oepen, Kristina Toutanova, Stuart Shieber, Christoper D. Manning, Dan Flickinger, and Thorsten Brant. 2002. The LinGO redwoods treebank: Motivation and preliminary applications. In *19th International Conference on Computational Linguistics: COLING-2002*, pages 1253–7. Taipei, Taiwan.

Ivan Sag, Timothy Baldwin, Francis Bond, Ann Copestake, and Dan Flickinger. 2002. Multiword expressions: A pain in the neck for NLP. In Alexander Gelbuk, editor, *Computational Linguistics and Intelligent Text Processing: Third International Conference: CICLing-2002*, pages 1–15. Springer-Verlag, Hiedelberg/Berlin.

Kiyoaki Shirai. 2002. Construction of a word sense tagged corpus for SENSEVAL-2 Japanese dictionary task. In *Third International Conference on Language Resources and Evaluation (LREC-2002)*, pages 605–608.

Benjamin Snyder and Martha Palmer. 2004. The English all-words task. In *Proceedings of Senseval-3*, pages 41–44. ACL, Barcelona.

Takaaki Tanaka, Francis Bond, Stephan Oepen, and Sanae Fujita. 2005. High precision treebanking – blazing useful trees using POS information. In *ACL-2005*, pages 330–337.

Ann Taylor, Mitchel Marcus, and Beatrice Santorini. 2003. The Penn treebank: an overview. In Abeillé (2003), chapter 1, pages 5–22.

Issues in Synchronizing the English Treebank and PropBank

Olga Babko-Malaya[a], Ann Bies[a], Ann Taylor[b], Szuting Yi[a], Martha Palmer[c], Mitch Marcus[a], Seth Kulick[a] and Libin Shen[a]

[a]University of Pennsylvania, [b]University of York, [c]University of Colorado

{malayao,bies}@ldc.upenn.edu, {szuting,mitch,skulick,libin}@linc.cis.upenn.edu, at9@york.ac.uk, Martha.Palmer@colorado.edu

Abstract

The PropBank primarily adds semantic role labels to the syntactic constituents in the parsed trees of the Treebank. The goal is for automatic semantic role labeling to be able to use the domain of locality of a predicate in order to find its arguments. In principle, this is exactly what is wanted, but in practice the PropBank annotators often make choices that do not actually conform to the Treebank parses. As a result, the syntactic features extracted by automatic semantic role labeling systems are often inconsistent and contradictory. This paper discusses in detail the types of mismatches between the syntactic bracketing and the semantic role labeling that can be found, and our plans for reconciling them.

1 Introduction

The PropBank corpus annotates the entire Penn Treebank with predicate argument structures by adding semantic role labels to the syntactic constituents of the Penn Treebank. Theoretically, it is straightforward for PropBank annotators to locate possible arguments based on the syntactic structure given by a parse tree, and mark the located constituent with its argument label. We would expect a one-to-one mapping between syntactic constituents and semantic arguments. However, in practice, PropBank annotators often make choices that do not actually conform to the Penn Treebank parses.

The discrepancies between the PropBank and the Penn Treebank obstruct the study of the syntax and semantics interface and pose an immediate problem to an automatic semantic role labeling system. A semantic role labeling system is trained on many syntactic features extracted from the parse trees, and the discrepancies make the training data inconsistent and contradictory. In this paper we discuss in detail the types of mismatches between the syntactic bracketing and the semantic role labeling that can be found, and our plans for reconciling them. We also investigate the sources of the disagreements, which types of disagreements can be resolved automatically, which types require manual adjudication, and for which types an agreement between syntactic and semantic representations cannot be reached.

1.1 Treebank

The Penn Treebank annotates text for syntactic structure, including syntactic argument structure and rough semantic information. Treebank annotation involves two tasks: part-of-speech tagging and syntactic annotation.

The first task is to provide a part-of-speech tag for every token. Particularly relevant for PropBank work, verbs in any form (active, passive, gerund, infinitive, etc.) are marked with a verbal part of speech (VBP, VBN, VBG, VB, etc.). (Marcus, et al. 1993; Santorini 1990)

The syntactic annotation task consists of marking constituent boundaries, inserting empty categories (traces of movement, PRO, pro), showing the relationships between constituents (argument/adjunct structures), and specifying a particular subset of adverbial roles. (Marcus, et al. 1994; Bies, et al. 1995)

Constituent boundaries are shown through syntactic node labels in the trees. In the simplest case, a node will contain an entire constituent, complete with any associated arguments or modifiers. However, in structures involving syntactic movement, sub-constituents may be displaced. In these cases, Treebank annotation represents the original position with a trace and shows the relationship as co-indexing. In (1) below, for example, the direct object of *entail* is shown with the trace *T*, which is coindexed to the WHNP node of the question word *what*.

```
(1) (SBARQ (WHNP-1 (WP What ))
        (SQ (VBZ does )
            (NP-SBJ (JJ industrial )
                    (NN emigration ))
            (VP (VB entail)
                (NP *T*-1)))
        (. ?))
```


Proceedings of the Workshop on Frontiers in Linguistically Annotated Corpora 2006, pages 70–77,
Sydney, July 2006.

In (2), the relative clause modifying *a journalist* has been separated from that NP by the prepositional phrase *to al Riyadh*, which is an argument of the verb *sent*. The position where the relative clause originated or "belongs" is shown by the trace *ICH*, which is coindexed to the SBAR node containing the relative clause constituent.

```
(2) (S (NP-SBJ You)
    (VP sent
        (NP (NP a journalist)
            (SBAR *ICH*-2))
        (PP-DIR to
                (NP al Riyadh))
        (SBAR-2
          (WHNP-3 who)
          (S (NP-SBJ *T*-3)
             (VP served
                 (NP (NP the name)
                     (PP of
                       (NP Lebanon)))
                 (ADVP-MNR
                   magnificently))))))
```

Empty subjects which are not traces of movement, such as PRO and pro, are shown as * (see the null subject of the infinite clause in (4) below). These null subjects are coindexed with a governing NP if the syntax allows. The null subject of an infinitive clause complement to a noun is, however, *not* coindexed with another node in the tree in the syntax. This coindexing is shown as a semantic coindexing in the PropBank annotation.

The distinction between syntactic arguments and adjuncts of the verb or verb phrase is made through the use of functional dashtags rather than with a structural difference. Both arguments and adjuncts are children of the VP node. No distinction is made between VP-level modification and S-level modification. All constituents that appear before the verb are children of S and sisters of VP; all constituents that appear after the verb are children of VP.

Syntactic arguments of the verb are NP-SBJ, NP (no dashtag), SBAR (either –NOM-SBJ or no dashtag), S (either –NOM-SBJ or no dashtag), -DTV, -CLR (closely/clearly related), -DIR with directional verbs.

Adjuncts or modifiers of the verb or sentence are any constituent with any other adverbial dashtag, PP (no dashtag), ADVP (no dashtag). Adverbial constituents are marked with a more specific functional dashtag if they belong to one of the more specific types in the annotation system (temporal –TMP, locative –LOC, manner –MNR, purpose –PRP, etc.).

Inside NPs, the argument/adjunct distinction is shown structurally. Argument constituents (S and SBAR only) are children of NP, sister to the head noun. Adjunct constituents are sister to the NP that contains the head noun, child of the NP that contains both:

```
(NP (NP head)
    (PP adjunct))
```

1.2 PropBank

PropBank is an annotation of predicate-argument structures on top of syntactically parsed, or Treebanked, structures. (Palmer, et al. 2005; Babko-Malaya, 2005). More specifically, PropBank annotation involves three tasks: argument labeling, annotation of modifiers, and creating co-reference chains for empty categories.

The first goal is to provide consistent argument labels across different syntactic realizations of the same verb, as in

(3) [ARG0 John] broke [ARG1 the window]
    [ARG1 The window] broke.

As this example shows, semantic arguments are tagged with numbered argument labels, such as Arg0, Arg1, Arg2, where these labels are defined on a verb by verb basis.

The second task of the PropBank annotation involves assigning functional tags to all modifiers of the verb, such as MNR (manner), LOC (locative), TMP (temporal), DIS (discourse connectives), PRP (purpose) or DIR (direction) and others.

And, finally, PropBank annotation involves finding antecedents for 'empty' arguments of the verbs, as in (4). The subject of the verb *leave* in this example is represented as an empty category [*] in Treebank. In PropBank, all empty categories which could be co-referred with a NP within the same sentence are linked in 'co-reference' chains:

(4) I made a decision [*] to leave

Rel: leave,
Arg0: [*] -> I

As the following sections show, all three tasks of PropBank annotation result in structures which differ in certain respects from the corresponding Treebank structures. Section 2 presents our approach to reconciling the differences between Treebank and PropBank with respect to the third task, which links empty categories with their antecedents. Section 3 introduces mismatches between syntactic constituency in Treebank and PropBank. Mismatches between modifier labels are not addressed in this paper and are left for future work.

2 Coreference and syntactic chains

PropBank chains include all syntactic chains (represented in the Treebank) plus other cases of nominal semantic coreference, including those in which the coreferring NP is not a syntactic antecedent. For example, according to PropBank guidelines, if a trace is coindexed with a NP in Treebank, then the chain should be reconstructed:

(5) What-1 do you like [*T*-1]?

Original PropBank annotation:
Rel: like
Arg0: you
Arg1: [*T*] -> What

Such chains usually include traces of A and A' movement and PRO for subject and object control. On the other hand, not all instances of PROs have syntactic antecedents. As the following example illustrates, subjects of infinitival verbs and gerunds might have antecedents within the same sentence, which cannot be linked as a syntactic chain.

(6) On the issue of abortion , Marshall Coleman wants to take away your right [*] to choose and give it to the politicians .

ARG0: [*] -> your
REL: choose

Given that the goal of PropBank is to find all semantic arguments of the verbs, the links between empty categories and their coreferring NPs are important, independent of whether they are syntactically coindexed or not. In order to reconcile the differences between Treebank and PropBank annotations, we decided to revise PropBank annotation and view it as a 3 stage process.

First, PropBank annotators should not reconstruct syntactic chains, but rather tag empty categories as arguments. For example, under the new approach annotators would simply tag the trace as the Arg1 argument in (7):

(7) What-1 do you like [*T*-1]?

Revised PropBank annotation:
Rel: like
Arg0: you
Arg1: [*T*]

As the second stage, syntactic chains will be reconstructed automatically, based on the coindexation provided by Treebank (note that the trace is coindexed with the NP *What* in (7)). And, finally, coreference annotation will be done on top of the resulting resource, with the goal of finding antecedents for the remaining empty categories, including empty subjects of infinitival verbs and gerunds.

One of the advantages of this approach is that it allows us to distinguish different types of chains, such as syntactic chains (i.e., chains which are derived as the result of syntactic movement, or control coreference), direct coreference chains (as illustrated by the example in (6)), and semantic type links for other 'indirect' types of links between an empty category and its antecedent.

Syntactic chains are annotated in Treebank, and are reconstructed automatically in PropBank. The annotation of direct coreference chains is done manually on top of Treebank, and is restricted to empty categories that are not coindexed with any NP in Treebank. And, finally, as we show next, a semantic type link is used for relative clauses and a coindex link for verbs of saying.

A semantic type link is used when the antecedent and the empty category do not refer to the same entity, but do have a certain kind of relationship. For example, consider the relative clause in (8):

(8) Answers that we'd like to have

Treebank annotation:
```
(NP (NP answers)
    (SBAR (WHNP-6 which)
          (S (NP-SBJ-3 we)
             (VP 'd
                (VP like
                   (S (NP-SBJ *-3)
                      (VP to
                         (VP have
                            (NP *T*-6)
    ))))))))
```

In Treebank, the object of the verb *have* is a trace, which is coindexed with the relative pronoun. In the original PropBank annotation, a further link is provided, which specifies the relative pronoun as being of "semantic type" *answers*.

(9) *Original PropBank annotation:*
Arg1: [NP *T*-6] -> which -> answers
rel: have
Arg0: [NP-SBJ *-3] -> we

This additional link between *which* and *answers* is important for many applications that make use of preferences for semantic types of verb arguments, such as Word Sense Disambiguation (Chen & Palmer 2005). In the new annotation scheme, annotators will first label traces as arguments:

(10) *Revised PropBank annotation (stage 1):*
Rel: have
Arg1: [*T*-6]
Arg0: [NP-SBJ *-3]

As the next stage, the trace [*T*-6] will be linked to the relative pronoun automatically (in addition to the chain *[NP-SBJ *-3] -> we* being automatically reconstructed). As the third stage, PropBank annotators will link *which* to *answers*. However, this chain will be labeled as a "semantic type" to distinguish it from direct coreference chains and to indicate that there is no identity relation between the coindexed elements.

Verbs of saying illustrate another case of links rather than coreference chains. In many sentences with direct speech, the clause which introduces a verb of saying is 'embedded' into the utterance. Syntactically this presents a problem for both Treebank and Propbank annotation. In Treebank, the original annotation style required a trace coindexed to the highest S node as the argument of the verb of saying, indicating syntactic movement.

(11) Among other things, they said [*T*-1] , Mr. Azoff would develop musical acts for a new record label .

Treebank annotation:

```
(S-1 (PP Among
        (NP other things))
    (PRN ,
      (S (NP-SBJ they)
         (VP said
            (SBAR 0
               (S *T*-1))))
         ,)
    (NP-SBJ Mr. Azoff)
    (VP would
      (VP develop
        (NP (NP musical acts)
            (PP for
               (NP a new record
                  label)))))
    .)
```

In PropBank, the different pieces of the utterance, including the trace under the verb *said*, were concatenated

(12) *Original PropBank annotation:*
ARG1: [Among other things] [Mr. Azoff] [would develop musical acts for a new record label] [[*T*-1]]
ARG0: they
rel: said

Under the new approach, in stage one, Treebank annotation will introduce not a trace of the S clause, but rather *?*, an empty category indicating ellipsis. In stage three, PropBank annotators will link this null element to the S node, but the resulting chain will not be viewed as 'direct' coreference. A special tag will be used for this link, in order to distinguish it from other types of chains.

(13) *Revised PropBank annotation:*
ARG1: [*?*] (-> S)
ARG0: they
rel: said

3 Differences in syntactic constituency

3.1 Extractions of mismatches between PropBank and Treebank

In order to make the necessary changes to both the Treebank and the PropBank, we have to first find all instances of mismatches. We have used two methods to do this: 1) examining the argument locations; 2) examining the discontinuous arguments.

Argument Locations In a parse tree which expresses the syntactic structure of a sentence, a semantic argument occupies specific syntactic locations: it appears in a subject position, a verb complement location or an adjunct location. Relative to the predicate, its argument is either a sister node, or a sister node of the predicate's ancestor. We extracted cases of PropBank arguments which do not attach to the predicate spine, and filtered out VP coordination cases. For example, the following case is a problematic one because the argument PP node is embedded too deeply in an NP node and hence it cannot find a connection with the main predicate verb *lifted*. This is an example of a PropBank annotation error.

(14)
```
(VP (VBD[rel] lifted)
      (NP us) )
      (NP-EXT
          (NP a good 12-inches)
          (PP-LOC[ARGM-LOC] above
              (NP the water level))))
```

However, the following case is not problematic because we consider the ArgM PP to be a sister node of the predicate verb given the VP coordination structure:

(15)
```
(VP (VP (VB[rel] buy)
        (NP the basket of … )
        (PP in whichever market …))
      (CC and)
      (VP (VBP sell)
        (NP them)
        (PP[ARGM] in the more
              expensive market)))
```

Discontinuous Arguments happen when PropBank annotators need to concatenate several Treebank constituents to form an argument. Discontinuous arguments often represent different opinions between PropBank and Treebank annotators regarding the interpretations of the sentence structure.

For example, in the following case, the PropBank concatenates the NP and the PP to be the Arg1. In this case, the disagreement on PP attachment is simply a Treebank annotation error.

(16) The region lacks necessary mechanisms for handling the aid and accounting items.

Treebank annotation:
```
(VP lacks
     (NP necessary mechanisms)
     (PP for
         (NP handing the aid…)))
```

PropBank annotation:
REL: lacks
Arg1: [NP necessary mechanisms][PP for handling the aid and accounting items]

All of these examples have been classified into the following categories: (1) attachment ambiguities, (2) different policy decisions, and (3) cases where one-to-one mapping cannot be preserved.

3.2 Attachment ambiguities

Many cases of mismatches between Treebank and PropBank constituents are the result of ambiguous interpretations. The most common examples are cases of modifier attachment ambiguities, including PP attachment. In cases of ambiguous interpretations, we are trying to separate cases which can be resolved automatically from those which require manual adjudication.

PP-Attachment The most typical case of PP attachment annotation disagreement is shown in (17).

(17) *She wrote a letter for Mary.*

Treebank annotation:
```
(VP wrote
     (NP (NP a letter)
         (PP for
             (NP Mary))))
```

PropBank annotation:
REL: write
Arg1: a letter
Arg2: for Mary

In (17), the PP 'for Mary' is attached to the verb in PropBank and to the NP in Treebank. This disagreement may have been influenced by the set of roles of the verb 'write', which includes a beneficiary as its argument.

(18) Frameset write:	Arg0: writer
	Arg1: thing written
	Arg2: beneficiary

Examples of this type cannot be automatically resolved and require manual adjudication.

Adverb Attachment Some cases of modifier attachment ambiguities, on the other hand, could be automatically resolved. Many cases of mismatches are of the type shown in (19), where a directional adverbial follows the verb. In Treebank, this adverbial is analyzed as part of an ADVP which is the argument of the verb in question. However, in PropBank, it is annotated as a separate ArgM-DIR.

(19) Everything is going back to Korea or Japan.

Treebank annotation:
```
(S (NP-SBJ (NN Everything) )
   (VP (VBZ is)
       (VP (VBG[rel] going)
           (ADVP-DIR
                (RB[ARGM-DIR] back)
                (PP[ARG2] (TO to)
                    (NP (NNP Korea)
                        (CC and)
                        (NNP Japan)
       ))))) (. .))
```

Original PropBank annotation:
Rel: going
ArgM-DIR: back
Arg2: to Korea or Japan

For examples of this type, we have decided to automatically reconcile PropBank annotations to be consistent with Treebank, as shown in (20).

(20) *Revised PropBank annotation:*
Rel: going
Arg2: back to Korea or Japan

3.3 Sentential complements

Another area of significant mismatch between Treebank and PropBank annotation involves sentential complements, both infinitival clauses and small clauses. In general, Treebank annotation allows many more verbs to take sentential complements than PropBank annotation.

For example, the Treebank annotation of the sentence in (21) gives the verb *keep* a sentential complement which has *their markets active* under the S as the subject of the complement clause. PropBank annotation, on the other hand, does not mark the clause but rather labels each subconstituent as a separate argument.

(21) …keep their markets active

Treebank annotation:
```
(VP keep
    (S (NP-SBJ their markets)
       (ADJP-PRD active)))
```

PropBank annotation:
REL: keep
Arg1: their markets
Arg2: active

In Propbank, an important criterion for deciding whether a verb takes an S argument, or decomposes it into two arguments (usually tagged as Arg1 and Arg2) is based on the semantic interpretation of the argument, e.g. whether the argument can be interpreted as an event or proposition.

For example, causative verbs (e.g. *make, get*), verbs of perception (*see, hear*), and intensional verbs (*want, need, believe*), among others, are analyzed as taking an S clause, which is interpreted as an event in the case of causative verbs and verbs of perception, and as a proposition in the case of intensional verbs. On the other hand, 'label' verbs (*name, call, entitle, label*, etc.), do not select for an event or proposition and are analyzed as having 3 arguments: Arg0, Arg1, and Arg2.

Treebank criteria for distinguishing arguments, on the other hand, were based on syntactic considerations, which did not always match with Propbank. For example, in Treebank, evidence of the syntactic category of argument that a verb can take is used as part of the decision process about whether to allow the verb to take a small clause. Verbs that take finite or non-finite (verbal) clausal arguments, are also treated as taking small clauses. The verb *find* takes a finite clausal complement as in *We found that the book was important* and also a non-finite clausal complement as in *We found the book to be important.* Therefore, *find* is also treated as taking a small clause complement as in *We found the book important.*

(22)
```
(S (NP-SBJ We)
   (VP found
       (S (NP-SBJ the book)
          (ADJP-PRD important))))
```

The obligatory nature of the secondary predicate in this construction also informed the decision to use a small clause with a verb like *find*. In (22), for example, *important* is an obligatory part of the sentence, and removing it makes the sentence ungrammatical with this sense of *find* ("We found the book" can only be grammatical with a different sense of *find*, essentially "We located the book").

With verbs that take infinitival clausal complements, however, the distinction between a single S argument and an NP object together with an S argument is more difficult to make. The original Treebank policy was to follow the criteria and the list of verbs taking both an NP object and an infinitival S argument given in Quirk, et al. (1985).

Resultative constructions are frequently a source of mismatch between Treebank annotation as a small clause and PropBank annotation with Arg1 and Arg2. Treebank treated a number of resultative as small clauses, although certain verbs received resultative structure annotation, such as the one in (23).

(23)
```
(S (NP-SBJ They)
   (VP painted
       (NP-1 the apartment)
       (S-CLR (NP-SBJ *-1)
              (ADJP-PRD orange))))
```

In all the mismatches in the area of sentential complementation, Treebank policy tends to overgeneralize S-clauses, whereas Propbank leans toward breaking down clauses into separate arguments.

This type of mismatch is being resolved on a verb-by-verb basis. Propbank will reanalyze some of the verbs (like *consider* and *find*), which have been analyzed as having 3 arguments, as taking an S argument. Treebank, on the other hand, will change the analysis of *label* verbs like *call*, from a small clause analysis to a structure with two complements.

Our proposed structure for *label* verbs, for example, is in (24).

(24)
```
(S (NP-SBJ[Arg0] his parents)
   (VP (VBD called)
       (NP-1[Arg1] him)
       (S-CLR[Arg2]
             (NP-SBJ *-1)
             (NP-PRD John))))
```

This structure will accommodate both Treebank and PropBank requirements for *label* verbs.

4 Where Syntax and Semantics do not match

Finally, there are some examples where the differences seem to be impossible to resolve without sacrificing some important features of PropBank or Treebank annotation.

4.1 Phrasal verbs

PropBank has around 550 phrasal verbs like *keep up*, *touch on*, *used to* and others, which are analyzed as separate predicates in PropBank. These verbs have their own set of semantic roles, which is different from the set of roles of the corresponding 'non-phrasal' verbs, and therefore they require a separate PropBank entry. In Treebank, on the other hand, phrasal verbs are not distinguished. If the second part of the phrasal verb is labeled as a verb+particle combination in the Treebank, the PropBank annotators concatenate it with the verb as the REL. If Treebank labels the second part of the 'phrasal verb' as part of a prepositional phrase, there is no way to resolve the inconsistency.

(25) But Japanese institutional investors are used to quarterly or semiannual payments on their investments, so ...

Treebank annotation:
```
(VBN used)
(PP (TO to)
    (NP quarterly or ...
        on their investments))
```

PropBank annotation:

Arg1: quarterly or ... on their investments
Rel: used to ('used to' is a separate predicate in PropBank)

4.2 Conjunction

In PropBank, conjoined NPs and clauses are usually analyzed as one argument, parallel to Treebank. For example, in *John and Mary came*, the NP *John and Mary* is a constituent in Treebank and it is also marked as Arg0 in PropBank. However, there are a few cases where one of the conjuncts is modified, and PropBank policy is to mark these modifiers as ArgMs. For example, in the following NP, the temporal ArgM *now* modifies a verb, but it only applies to the second conjunct.

(26)
```
(NP (NNP Richard)
    (NNP Thornburgh) )
(, ,)
(SBAR
  (WHNP-164 (WP who))
  (S
    (NP-SBJ-1 (-NONE- *T*-164))
    (VP
      (VBD went)
      (PRT (RP on) )
      (S
        (NP-SBJ (-NONE- *-1))
        (VP (TO to)
          (VP (VB[rel] become)
            (NP-PRD
              (NP[ARG2]
                (NP (NN governor))
                (PP (IN of)
                 (NP
                  (NNP
                   Pennsylvania))))
```

```
(CC and)
(PRN (, ,)
  (ADVP-TMP (RB now))
    (, ,) )
(NP[ARG2] (NNP U.S.)
        (NNP Attorney)
        (NNP General))
)))))))
```

In PropBank, cases like this can be decomposed into two propositions:

(27) Prop1: rel: become
Arg1: attorney general
Arg0: [-NONE- *-1]

Prop2: rel: become
ArgM-TMP: now
Arg0: [-NONE- *-1]
Arg1: a governor

In Treebank, the conjoined NP is necessarily analyzed as one constituent. In order to maintain the one-to-one mapping between PropBank and Treebank, PropBank annotation would have to be revised in order to allow the sentence to have one proposition with a conjoined phrase as an argument. Fortunately, these types of cases do not occur frequently in the corpus.

4.3 Gapping

Another place where the one-to-one mapping is difficult to preserve is with gapping constructions. Treebank annotation does not annotate the gap, given that gaps might correspond to different syntactic categories or may not even be a constituent. The policy of Treebank, therefore, is simply to provide a coindexation link between the corresponding constituents:

(28) Mary-1 likes chocolates-2 and
Jane=1 – flowers=2

This policy obviously presents a problem for one-to-one mapping, since Propbank annotators tag *Jane* and *flowers* as the arguments of an implied second *likes* relation, which is not present in the sentence.

5 Summary

In this paper we have considered several types of mismatches between the annotations of the English Treebank and the PropBank: coreference and syntactic chains, differences in syntactic constituency, and cases in which syntax and semantics do not match. We have found that for the most part, such mismatches arise because Treebank decisions are based primarily on syntactic considerations while PropBank decisions give more weight to semantic representation..

In order to reconcile these differences we have revised the annotation policies of both the PropBank and Treebank in appropriate ways. A fourth source of mismatches is simply annotation error in either the Treebank or PropBank. Looking at the mismatches in general has allowed us to find these errors, and will facilitate their correction.

References

Olga Babko-Malaya. 2005. *PropBank Annotation Guidelines.* http://www.cis.upenn.edu/~mpalmer/project_pages/PBguidelines.pdf

Ann Bies, Mark Ferguson, Karen Katz, Robert MacIntyre. 1995. *Bracketing Guidelines for Treebank II Style*. Penn Treebank Project, University of Pennsylvania, Department of Computer and Information Science Technical Report MS-CIS-95-06.

Jinying Chen and Martha Palmer. 2005. Towards Robust High Performance Word Sense Disambiguation of English Verbs Using Rich Linguistic Features. In *Proceedings of the 2nd International Joint Conference on Natural Language Processing, IJCNLP2005*, pp. 933-944. Oct. 11-13, Jeju Island, Republic of Korea.

M. Marcus, G. Kim, M. Marcinkiewicz, R. MacIntyre, A. Bies, M. Ferguson, K. Katz & B. Schasberger, 1994. The Penn Treebank: Annotating predicate argument structure. *Proceedings of the Human Language Technology Workshop*, San Francisco.

M. Marcus, B. Santorini and M.A. Marcinkiewicz, 1993. Building a large annotated corpus of English: the Penn Treebank. *Computational Linguistics.*

Martha Palmer, Dan Gildea, and Paul Kingsbury. 2005. The proposition bank: An annotated corpus of semantic roles. *Computational Linguistics,* 31(1).

R. Quirk, S. Greenbaum, G. Leech and J. Svartvik. 1985. *A Comprehensive Grammar of the English Language*. Longman, London.

B. Santorini. 1990. *Part-of-speech tagging guidelines for the Penn Treebank Project.* University of Pennsylvania, Department of Computer and Information Science Technical Report MS-CIS-90-47.

On Distance between Deep Syntax and Semantic Representation

Václav Novák
Institute of Formal and Applied Linguistics
Charles University
Praha, Czech Republic
novak@ufal.mff.cuni.cz

Abstract

We present a comparison of two formalisms for representing natural language utterances, namely deep syntactical *Tectogrammatical Layer* of Functional Generative Description (FGD) and a semantic formalism, *MultiNet*. We discuss the possible position of MultiNet in the FGD framework and present a preliminary mapping of representational means of these two formalisms.

1 Introduction

The Prague Dependency Treebank 2.0 (PDT 2.0) described in Sgall et al. (2004) contains a large amount of Czech texts with complex and interlinked morphological (2 million words), syntactic (1.5M words), and complex semantic (tectogrammatical) annotation (0.8M words); in addition, certain properties of sentence information structure and coreference relations are annotated at the semantic level.

The theoretical basis of the treebank lies in the Functional Generative Description (FGD) of language system by Sgall et al. (1986).

PDT 2.0 is based on the long-standing Praguian linguistic tradition, adapted for the current computational-linguistics research needs. The corpus itself is embedded into the latest annotation technology. Software tools for corpus search, annotation, and language analysis are included. Extensive documentation (in English) is provided as well.

An example of a tectogrammatical tree from PDT 2.0 is given in figure 1. Function words are removed, their function is preserved in node attributes (*grammatemes*), information structure is annotated in terms of topic-focus articulation, and every node receives detailed semantic label corresponding to its function in the utterance (e.g., *addressee*, *from_where*, *how_often*, ...). The square node indicates an obligatory but missing valent. The tree represents the following sentence:

Letos se snaží o návrat do politiky.
This year he tries to return to politics. (1)

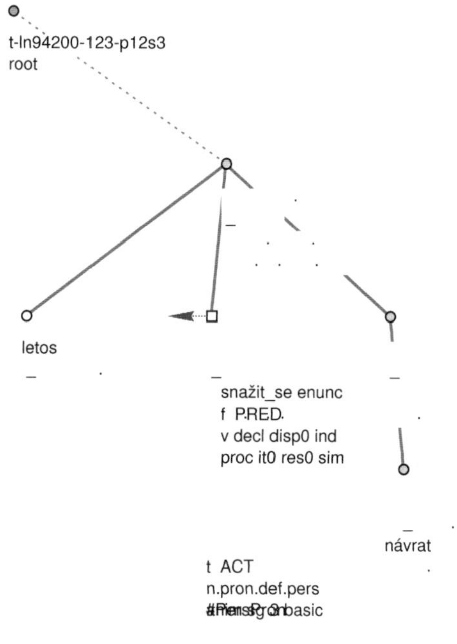

Figure 1: Tectogrammatical tree of sentence (1)

1.1 MultiNet

The representational means of Multilayered Extended Semantic Networks (MultiNet), which are

Proceedings of the Workshop on Frontiers in Linguistically Annotated Corpora 2006, pages 78–85,
Sydney, July 2006.

described in Helbig (2006), provide a universally applicable formalism for treatment of semantic phenomena of natural language. To this end, they offer distinct advantages over the use of the classical predicate calculus and its derivatives. The knowledge representation paradigm and semantic formalism MultiNet is used as a common backbone for all aspects of natural language processing (be they theoretical or practical ones). It is continually used for the development of intelligent information and communication systems and for natural language interfaces to the Internet. Within this framework, it is subject to permanent practical evaluation and further development.

The semantic representation of natural language expressions by means of MultiNet is mainly independent of the considered language. In contrast, the syntactic constructs used in different languages to describe the same content are obviously not identical. To bridge the gap between different languages we can employ the deep syntactico-semantic representation available in the FGD framework.

An example of a MultiNet structure is given in figure 2. The figure represents the following discourse:

Max gave his brother several apples.
This was a generous gift.
Four of them were rotten. (2)

MultiNet is not explicitly model-theoretical and the extensional level is created only in those situations where the natural language expressions require it. It can be seen that the overall structure of the representation is not a tree unlike in Tectogrammatical representation (TR). The layer information is hidden except for the most important QUANT and CARD values. These attributes convey information that is important with respect to the content of the sentence. TR lacks attributes distinguishing intensional and extensional information and there are no relations like SUBM denoting relation between a set and its subset.

Note that the MultiNet representation crosses the sentence boundaries. First, the structure representing a sentence is created and then this structure is assimilated into the existing representation.

In contrast to CLASSIC (Brachman et al., 1991) and other KL-ONE networks, MultiNet contains a predefined final set of relation types, encapsulation of concepts, and attribute layers concerning cardinality of objects mentioned in discourse.

In Section 2, we describe our motivation for extending the annotation in FGD to an even deeper level. Section 3 lists the MultiNet structural counterparts of tectogrammatical means. We discuss the related work in Section 4. Section 5 deals with various evaluation techniques and we conclude in Section 6.

2 FGD layers

PDT 2.0 contains three layers of information about the text (as described in Hajič (1998)):

Morphosyntactic Tagging. This layer represents the text in the original linear word order with a tag assigned unambiguously to each word form occurence, much like the Brown corpus does.

Syntactic Dependency Annotation. It contains the (unambiguous) dependency representation of every sentence, with features describing the morphosyntactic properties, the syntactic function, and the lexical unit itself. All words from the sentence appear in its representation.

Tectogrammatical Representation (TR). At this level of description, we annotate every (autosemantic non-auxiliary) lexical unit with its tectogrammatical function, position in the scale of the communicative dynamism and its grammatemes (similar to the morphosyntactic tag, but only for categories which cannot be derived from the word's function, like number for nouns, but not its case).

There are several reasons why TR may not be sufficient in a question answering system or MT:

1. The syntactic functors Actor and Patient disallow creating inference rules for cognitive roles like *Affected object* or *State carrier*. For example, the axiom stating that an affected object is changed by the event $((v \text{ AFF } o) \rightarrow (v \text{ SUBS } \texttt{change.2.1}))$ can not be used in the TR framework.

2. There is no information about sorts of concepts represented by TR nodes. Sorts (the upper conceptual ontology) are an important source of constraints for MultiNet relations. Every relation has its signature which in turn

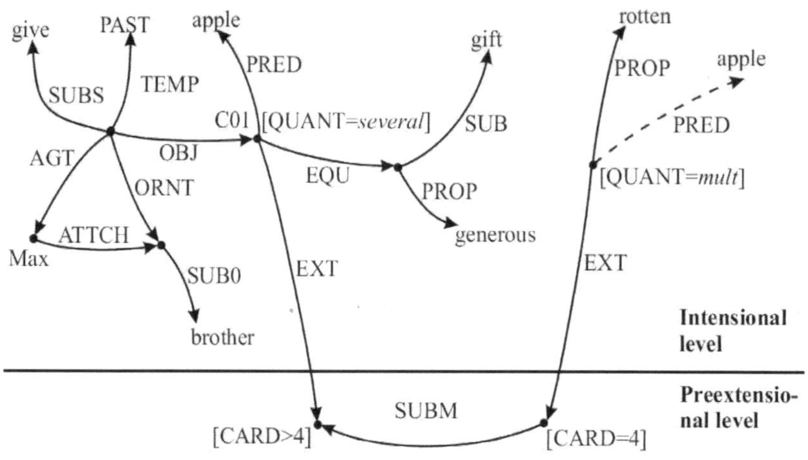

Figure 2: MultiNet representation of example discourse (2)

reduces ambiguity in the process of text analysis and inferencing.

3. Lexemes of TR have no hierarchy which limits especially the search for an answer in a question answering system. In TR there is no counterpart of SUB, SUBR, and SUBS MultiNet relations which connect subordinate concepts to superordinate ones and individual object representatves to corresponding generic concepts.

4. In TR, each sentence is isolated from the rest of the text, except for coreference arrows heading to preceding sentences. This, in effect, disallows inferences combining knowledge from multiple sentences in one inference rule.

5. Nodes in TR always correspond to a word or a group of words in the surface form of sentence or to a deleted obligatory valency of another node. There are no means for representing knowledge generated during the inference process, if the knowledge doesn't have a form of TR. For example, consider axiom of temporal precedence transitivity (3):

$$(a \text{ ANTE } b) \wedge (b \text{ ANTE } c) \rightarrow (a \text{ ANTE } c) \quad (3)$$

In TR, we can not add an edge denoting $(a \text{ ANTE } c)$. We would have to include a proposition like "a precedes c" as a whole new clause.

For all these reasons we need to extend our text annotation to a form suitable to more advanced tasks. It is shown in Helbig (2006) that MultiNet is capable to solve all the above mentioned issues.

Helbig (1986) describes a procedure for automatic translation of natural language utterances into MultiNet structures used in WOCADI tool for German. WOCADI uses no theoretical intermediate structures and relies heavily on semantically annotated dictionary (HagenLex, see Hartrumpf et al. (2003)).

In our approach, we want to take advantage of existing tools for conversions between layers in FGD. By combining several simpler procedures for translation between adjacent layers, we can improve the robustness of the whole procedure and the modularity of the software tools. Moreover, the process is divided to logical steps corresponding to theoretically sound and well defined structures. On the other hand, such a multistage processing is susceptible to accumulation of errors made by individual components.

3 Structural Similarities

3.1 Nodes and Concepts

If we look at examples of TR and MultiNet structures, at first sight we can see that the nodes of TR mostly correspond to concepts in MultiNet. However, there is a major difference: TR does not include the concept encapsulation. The encapsulation in MultiNet serves for distinguishing definitional knowledge from assertional knowledge about given node, e.g., in the sentence "The old man is sleeping", the connection to *old* will be in the definitional part of *man*, while the connection to the state *is sleeping* belongs to the assertional part of the concept representing the *man*. In TR, these differences in content are represented by differences in Topic-Focus Articulation (TFA) of corresponding words.

There are also TR nodes that correspond to no MultiNet concept (typically, the node representing the verb "be") and TR nodes corresponding to a whole subnetwork, e.g., *Fred* in the sentence "Fred is going home.", where the TR node representing *Fred* corresponds to the subnetwork[1] in figure 3.

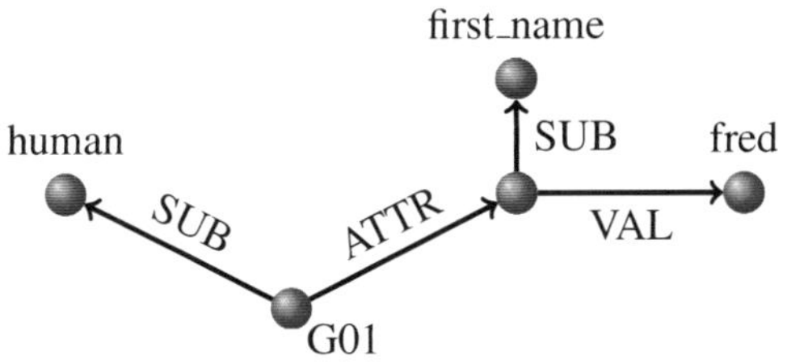

Figure 3: The MultiNet subnetwork corresponding to TR node representing *Fred*

3.2 Edges, relations and functions

An edge of TR between nodes that have their conceptual counterparts in MultiNet always corresponds to one or more relations and possibly also some functions. In general, it can be said that MultiNet representation of a text contains significantly more connections (either as relations, or as functions) than TR, and some of them correspond to TR edges.

3.3 Functors and types of relations and functions

There are 67 functor types in TR (see Hajičová et al. (2000) for description), which correspond to 94 relation types and 19 function types in MultiNet (Helbig, 2006). The mapping of TR functions to MultiNet is given in table 1:

TR functor	MultiNet counterpart
ACMP	ASSOC
ACT	AFF, AGT, BENF, CSTR, EXP, MEXP, SCAR
ADDR	ORNT
ADVS	SUBST, OPPOS
AIM	PURP
APP	ASSOC, ATTCH

continued ...

[1]In fact the concept representing the man is the concept G01, i.e. only one vertex. However, the whole network corresponds to the TR node representing *Fred*.

TR functor	MultiNet counterpart
APPS	EQU, NAME
ATT	MODL
AUTH	AGT, ORIG
BEN	BENF
CAUS	CAUS, JUST
CNCS	CONC
CM	*ITMS, MODL
COMPL	PROP except for sentential complements
COND	COND
CONFR	OPPOS
CONJ	*IMTS-I, *TUPL
CONTRA	OPPOS
CONTRD	CONC
CPR	*COMP
CRIT	METH, JUST, CIRC, CONF
CSQ	CAUS, JUST, GOAL
DIFF	*MODP, *OP
DIR1	ORIGL, ORIG
DIR2	VIA
DIR3	DIRCL, ELMT
DISJ	*ALTN2, *VEL2
EFF	MCONT, PROP, RSLT
EXT	QMOD
HER	AVRT
ID	NAME
INTT	PURP
LOC	LOC, LEXT
MANN	MANNR, METH
MAT	ORIGM
MEANS	MODE, INSTR
MOD	MODL
OPER	*OP, TEMP
ORIG	AVRT, INIT, ORIGM, ORIGL, ORIG
PARTL	MODL
PAT	AFF, ATTR, BENF, ELMT, GOAL, OBJ, PARS, PROP, SSPE, VAL
PREC	REAS, OPPOS
REAS	CAUS, GOAL
REG	CONF
RESL	CAUS, GOAL
RESTR	*DIFF
RHEM	MODL
RSTR	PROP, ATTR
SUBS	SUBST

continued ...

TR functor	MultiNet counterpart
TFHL	DUR
TFRWH	TEMP
THL	DUR
THO	QUANT layer
TOWH	SUBST, TEMP
TPAR	TEMP, DUR
TSIN	STRT
TTILL	FIN
TWHEN	TEMP

Table 1: Mapping of TR functors to MultiNet

There are also TR functors with no appropriate MultiNet counterpart: CPHR, DENOM, DPHR, FPHR, GRAD, INTF, PAR, PRED and VOCAT

Table 2 shows the mapping from MultiNet relations to TR functors:

MultiNet	TR counterpart
Relations:	
AFF	PAT, DIR1
AGT	ACT
ANTE	TWHEN
ARG1/2/3	ACT, PAT, ...
ASSOC	ACMP, APP
ATTCH	APP
ATTR	RSTR
AVRT	ORIG, ADDR, DIR1
BENF	BEN
CAUS	CAUS, RESL, REAS, GOAL
CIRC	CRIT
CONC	CNCS
COND	COND
CONF	REG, CRIT
CSTR	ACT
CTXT	REG
DIRCL	DIR3
DUR	TFHL, PAR, THL
ELMT	DIR3, DIR1
EXP	ACT
FIN	TTILL
GOAL	see RSLT, DIRCL and PURP
IMPL	CAUS
INIT	ORIG
INSTR	MEANS
JUST	CAUS
LEXT	LOC
LOC	LOC
MANNR	MANN

continued ...

MultiNet	TR counterpart
MCONT	PAT, EFF
MERO	see PARS, ORIGM, *ELMT, *SUBM and TEMP
METH	MANN, CRIT
MEXP	ACT
MODE	see INSTR, METH and MANNR
MODL	MOD, ATT, PARTL, RHEM
NAME	ID, APPS
OBJ	PAT
OPPOS	CONTRA
ORIG	ORIG, DIR1, AUTH
ORIGL	DIR1
ORIGM	ORIG
ORNT	ADDR
PROP	COMPL, RSTR
PROPR	COMPL, RSTR
PURP	AIM
QMOD	RSTR
REAS	see CAUS, JUST and IMPL
RPRS	LOC, MANN
RSLT	PAT, EFF
SCAR	ACT
SITU	see CIRC and CTXT
SOURC	see INIT, ORIG, ORIGL, ORIGM and AVRT
SSPE	PAT
STRT	TSIN
SUBST	SUBS
SUPPL	PAT
TEMP	TWHEN
VAL	RSTR, PAT
VIA	DIR2
Functions:	
*ALTN1	CONJ
*ALTN1	DISJ
*COMP	CPR, grammateme DEGCMP
*DIFF	RESTR
*INTSC	CONJ
*ITMS	CONJ
*MODP	MANN
*MODQ	RHEM
*MODS	MANNR
*NON	grammateme NEGATION
*ORD	grammateme NUMERTYPE
*PMOD	RSTR
*QUANT	MAT, RSTR

continued ...

MultiNet	TR counterpart
*SUPL	grammateme DEGCMP
*TUPL	CONJ
*UNION	CONJ
*VEL1	CONJ
*VEL2	DISJ

Table 2: Mapping of MultiNet relations to TR

There are also MultiNet relations and functions with no counterpart in TR (stars at the beginning denote a function): ANLG, ANTO, CHEA, CHPA, CHPE, CHPS, CHSA CHSP, CNVRS, COMPL, CONTR, CORR, DISTG, DPND, EQU, EXT, HSIT, MAJ, MIN, PARS, POSS, PRED0, PRED, PREDR, PREDS, SETOF, SUB, SYNO, VALR, *FLPJ and *OP.

From the tables 1 and 2, we can conclude that although the mapping is not one to one, the preprocessing of the input text to TR highly reduces the problem of the appropriate text to MultiNet transformation. However, it is not clear how to solve the remaining ambiguity.

3.4 Grammatemes and layer information

TR has at its disposal 15 grammatemes, which can be conceived as node attributes. Note that not all grammatemes are applicable to all nodes. The grammatemes in TR roughly correspond to layer information in MultiNet, but also to specific MultiNet relations.

1. NUMBER. This TR grammateme is transformed to QUANT, CARD, and ETYPE attributes in MultiNet.

2. GENDER. This syntactical information is not transformed to the semantic representation with the exception of occurences where the grammateme distinguishes the gender of an animal or a person and where MultiNet uses SUB relation with appropriate concepts.

3. PERSON. This verbal grammateme is reflected in cognitive roles connected to the event or state and is semantically superfluous.

4. POLITENESS has no structural counterpart in MultiNet. It can be represented in the conceptual hierarchy of SUB relation.

5. NUMERTYPE distinguishing e.g. "three" from "third" and "one third" is transformed to corresponding number and also to the manner this number is connected to the network.

6. INDEFTYPE corresponds to QUANT and VARIA layer attributes.

7. NEGATION is transformed to both FACT layer attribute and *NON function combined with modality relation.

8. DEGCMP corresponds to *COMP and *SUPL functions.

9. VERBMOD: *imp* value is represented by MODL relation to imperative, *cdn* value is ambiguous not only with respect to facticity of the condition but also with regard to other criteria distinguishing CAUS, IMPL, JUST and COND relatinos which can all result in a sentence with *cdn* verb. Also the FACT layer attribute of several concepts is affected by this value.

10. DEONTMOD corresponds to MODL relation.

11. DISPMOD is semantically superfluous.

12. ASPECT has no direct counterpart in MultiNet. It can be represented by the interplay of temporal specification and RSLT relation connecting an action to its result.

13. TENSE is represented by relations ANTE, TEMP, DUR, STRT, and FIN.

14. RESULTATIVE has no direct counterpart and must be expressed using the RSLT relation.

15. ITERATIVENESS should be represented by a combination of DUR and TEMP relations where some of temporal concepts have QUANT layer information set to *several*.

3.5 TFA, quantifiers, and encapsulation

In TR, the information structure of every utterance is annotated in terms of Topic-Focus Articulation (TFA):

1. Every autosemantic word is marked `c`, `t`, or `f` for contrastive topic, topic, or focus, respectively. The values can distinguish which part of the sentence belongs to topic and which part to focus.

2. There is an ordering of all nodes according to communicative dynamism (CD). Nodes with lower values of CD belong to topic and nodes

with greater values to focus. In this way, the degree of "aboutness" is distinguished even inside topic and focus of sentences.

MultiNet, on the other hand, doesn't contain any representational means devoted directly to representation of information structure. Nevertheless, the differences in the content of sentences differing only in TFA can be represented in MultiNet by other means. The TFA differences can be reflected in these categories:

- Relations connecting the topic of sentence with the remaining concepts in the sentence are usually a part of definitional knowledge about the concepts in the topic, while the relations going to the focus belong to the assertional part of knowledge about the concepts in focus. In other words, TFA can be reflected in different values of K_TYPE attribute.

- TFA has an effect on the identification of presuppositions (Peregrin, 1995a) and allegations (Hajičová, 1984). In case of presupposition, we need to know about them in the process of assimilation of new information into the existing network in order to detect presupposition failures. In case of allegation, there is a difference in FACT attribute of the allegation.

- The TFA has an influence on the scope of quantifiers (Peregrin, 1995b; Hajičová et al., 1998). This information is fully transformed into the quantifier scopes in MultiNet.

4 Related Work

There are various approaches trying to analyze text to a semantic representation. Some of them use layered approach and others use only a single tool to directly produce the target structure. For German, there is the above mentioned WOCADI parser to MultiNet, for English, there is a Discourse Representation Theory (DRT) analyzer (Bos, 2005), and for Czech there is a Transparent Intensional Logic analyzer (Horák, 2001).

The layered approaches: DeepThought project (Callmeier et al., 2004) can combine output of various tools into one representation. It would be even possible to incorporate TR and MultiNet into this framework. Meaning-Text Theory (Bolshakov and Gelbukh, 2000) uses an approach similar to Functional Generative Description (Žabokrtský, 2005) but it also has no layer corresponding to MultiNet.

There were attempts to analyze the semantics of TR, namely in question answering system TIBAQ (Jirků and Hajič, 1982), which used TR directly as the semantic representation, and Kruijff-Korbayová (1998), who tried to transform the TFA information in TR into the DRT framework.

5 Evaluation

It is a still open question how to evaluate systems for semantic representation. Basically, three approaches are used in similar projects:

First, the **coverage** of the system may serve as a basis for evaluation. This criterion is used in several systems (Bos, 2005; Horák, 2001; Callmeier et al., 2004). However, this criterion is far from ideal, because it's not applicable to robust systems and can not tell anything about the quality of resulting representation.

Second, the **consistency** of the semantic representation serves as an evaluation criterion in Bos (2005). It is a desired state to have a consistent representation of texts, but there is no guarantee that a consistent semantic representation is in any sense also a good one.

Third, the **performance in an application** (e.g., question answering system) is another criterion used for evaluating a semantic representation (Hartrumpf, 2005). A problem in this kind of evaluation is that we can not separate the evaluation of the formalism itself from the evaluation of the automatic processing tools. This problem becomes even bigger in a multilayered approach like FGD or MTT, where the overall performance depends on all participating transducers as well as on the quality of the theoretical description. However, from the user point of view, this is so far the most reliable form of semantic representation evaluation.

6 Conclusion

We have presented an outline of a procedure that enables us to transform syntactical (tectogrammatical) structures into a fully equipped knowledge representation framework. We have compared the structural properties of TR and MultiNet and found both similarities and differences suggesting which parts of such a task are more difficult and which are rather technical. The comparison shows that for applications requiring understanding of texts (e.g., question answering system) it is desirable to further analyze TR into another layer of knowledge representation.

Acknowledgement

This work was supported by Czech Academy of Science grant 1ET201120505 and by Czech Ministry of Education, Youth and Sports project LC536. The views expressed are not necessarily endorsed by the sponsors. We also thank anonymous reviewers for improvements in the final version.

References

Igor Bolshakov and Alexander Gelbukh. 2000. The Meaning-Text Model: Thirty Years After. *International Forum on Information and Documentation*, 1:10–16.

Johan Bos. 2005. Towards Wide-Coverage Semantic Interpretation. In *Proceedings of Sixth International Workshop on Computational Semantics IWCS-6*, pages 42–53.

Ronald J. Brachman, Deborah L. McGuinness, Peter F. Patel-Schneider, Lori Alperin Resnick, and Alex Borgida. 1991. Living with CLASSIC: When and How to Use a KL-ONE-like Language. In John Sowa, editor, *Principles of Semantic Networks: Explorations in the representation of knowledge*, pages 401–456. Morgan-Kaufmann, San Mateo, California.

Ulrich Callmeier, Andreas Eisele, Ulrich Schäfer, and Melanie Siegel. 2004. The DeepThought Core Architecture Framework. In *Proceedings of LREC*, May.

Jan Hajič. 1998. Building a Syntactically Annotated Corpus: The Prague Dependency Treebank. In E. Hajičová, editor, *Issues of Valency and Meaning. Studies in Honour of Jarmila Panevová*, pages 106–132. Karolinum, Charles University Press, Prague, Czech Republic.

Eva Hajičová, Jarmila Panevová, and Petr Sgall. 2000. A Manual for Tectogrammatic Tagging of the Prague Dependency Treebank. Technical Report TR-2000-09, ÚFAL MFF UK, Prague, Czech Republic. in Czech.

Eva Hajičová, Petr Sgall, and Barbara Partee. 1998. *Topic-Focus Articulation, Tripartite Structures, and Semantic Content*. Kluwer, Dordrecht.

Eva Hajičová. 1984. Presupposition and Allegation Revisited. *Journal of Pragmatics*, 8:155–167.

Sven Hartrumpf, Hermann Helbig, and Rainer Osswald. 2003. The Semantically Based Computer Lexicon HaGenLex – Structure and Technological Environment. *Traitement automatique des langues*, 44(2):81–105.

Sven Hartrumpf. 2005. University of hagen at qa@clef 2005: Extending knowledge and deepening linguistic processing for question answering. In Carol Peters, editor, *Results of the CLEF 2005 Cross-Language System Evaluation Campaign, Working Notes for the CLEF 2005 Workshop*, Wien, Österreich. Centromedia.

Hermann Helbig. 1986. Syntactic-Semantic Analysis of Natural Language by a New Word-Class Controlled Functional Analysis. *Computers and Artificial Inteligence*, 5(1):53–59.

Hermann Helbig. 2006. *Knowledge Representation and the Semantics of Natural Language*. Springer-Verlag, Berlin Heidelberg.

Aleš Horák. 2001. *The Normal Translation Algorithm in Transparent Intensional Logic for Czech*. Ph.D. thesis, Faculty of Informatics, Masaryk University, Brno, Czech Republic.

Petr Jirků and Jan Hajič. 1982. Inferencing and search for an answer in TIBAQ. In *Proceedings of the 9th conference on Computational linguistics – Volume 2*, pages 139–141, Prague, Czechoslovakia.

Ivana Kruijff-Korbayová. 1998. *The Dynamic Potential of Topic and Focus: A Praguian Approach to Discourse Representation Theory*. Ph.D. thesis, ÚFAL, MFF UK, Prague, Czech Republic.

Jaroslav Peregrin. 1995a. Topic, Focus and the Logic of Language. In *Sprachtheoretische Grundlagen für die Computerlinguistik (Proceedings of the Goettingen Focus Workshop, 17. DGfS)*, Heidelberg. IBM Deutschland.

Jaroslav Peregrin. 1995b. Topic-Focus Articulation as Generalized Quantification. In P. Bosch and R. van der Sandt, editors, *Proceedings of "Focus and natural language processing"*, pages 49–57, Heidelberg. IBM Deutschland.

Petr Sgall, Eva Hajičová, and Jarmila Panevová. 1986. *The Meaning of the Sentence in Its Semantic and Pragmatic Aspects*. D. Reidel Publishing company, Dodrecht, Boston, London.

Petr Sgall, Jarmila Panevová, and Eva Hajičová. 2004. Deep Syntactic Annotation: Tectogrammatical Representation and Beyond. In A. Meyers, editor, *Proceedings of the HLT-NAACL 2004 Workshop: Frontiers in Corpus Annotation*, pages 32–38, Boston, Massachusetts, USA. Association for Computational Linguistics.

Zdeněk Žabokrtský. 2005. Resemblances between Meaning-Text Theory and Functional Generative Description. In *Proceedings of the 2nd International Conference of Meaning-Text Theory*, pages 549–557.

Corpus annotation by generation

Elke Teich
TU Darmstadt
Darmstadt, Germany
teich@linglit.tu-darmstadt.de

John A. Bateman
Universität Bremen
Bremen, Germany
bateman@uni-bremen.de

Richard Eckart
TU Darmstadt
Darmstadt, Germany
eckart@linglit.tu-darmstadt.de

Abstract

As the interest in annotated corpora is spreading, there is increasing concern with using existing language technology for corpus processing. In this paper we explore the idea of using natural language *generation* systems for corpus annotation. Resources for generation systems often focus on areas of linguistic variability that are under-represented in analysis-directed approaches. Therefore, making use of generation resources promises some significant extensions in the kinds of annotation information that can be captured. We focus here on exploring the use of the KPML (Komet-Penman MultiLingual) generation system for corpus annotation. We describe the kinds of linguistic information covered in KPML and show the steps involved in creating a standard XML corpus representation from KPML's generation output.

1 Introduction

Many high-quality, theory-rich language processing systems can potentially be applied to corpus processing. However, the application of existing language technology, such as lexical and/or grammatical resources as well as parsers, turns out not to be as straightforward as one might think it should be. Using existing computational lexicons or thesauri, for instance, can be of limited value because they do not contain the domain-specific vocabulary that is needed for a particular corpus. Similarly, most existing grammatical resources for parsing have restricted *coverage* in precisely those areas of variation that are now most in need of corpus-supported investigation (e.g., predicate-argument structure, information structure, rhetorical structure). Apart from limited coverage, further issues that may impede the ready application of parsers in corpus processing include:

- *Annotation relevance.* Specialized, theory-specific parsers (also called 'deep parsers'; e.g., LFG or HPSG parsers) have been built with theoretical concerns in mind rather than appliability to unrestricted text. They may thus produce information that is not annotationally relevant (e.g., many logically equivalent readings of a single clause).

- *Usability.* Deep parsers are highly complex tools that require expert knowledge. The effort in acquiring this expert knowledge may be too high relative to the corpus processing task.

- *Completeness.* Simple parsers (commonly called 'shallow parsers'), on the other hand, produce only one type of annotationally relevant information (e.g., PoS, phrase/dependency structure). Other desirable kinds of information are thus lacking (e.g., syntactic functions, semantic roles, theme-rheme).

- *Output representation.* Typically, a parsing output is represented in a theory-specific way (e.g., in the case of LFG or HPSG parsers, a feature structure). Such output does not conform to the common practices in corpus representation.[1] Thus, it has to be mapped onto one of the standardly used data models for corpora (e.g., annotation graphs (Bird and Liberman, 2001) or multi-layer hierarchies (Sperberg-McQueen and Huitfeldt, 2001; Teich et al., 2001)) and transformed to a commonly employed format, typically XML.

[1] This is in contrast to the output representation of shallow parsers which have often been developed with the goal of corpus processing.

Proceedings of the Workshop on Frontiers in Linguistically Annotated Corpora 2006, pages 86–93,
Sydney, July 2006.

In spite of these difficulties, there is a general consensus that the reward for exploring deep processing techniques to build up small to medium-scale corpus resources lies in going beyond the kinds of linguistic information typically covered by treebanks (cf. (Baldwin et al., 2004; Cahill et al., 2002; Frank et al., 2003)).

In this paper, we would like to contribute to this enterprise by adding a novel, yet complementary perspective on theory-rich, high-quality corpus annotation. In a reappraisal of the potential contribution of natural language generation technology for providing richly annotated corpora, we explore the idea of annotation by generation. Although this may at first glance seem counter-intuitive, in fact a generator, similar to a parser, creates rather complex linguistic descriptions (which are ultimately realized as strings). In our current investigations, we are exploring the use of these complex linguistic descriptions for creating annotations. We believe that this may offer a worthwhile alternative or extension of corpus annotation methods which may alleviate some of the problems encountered in parsing-based approaches.

The generation system we are using is the KPML (Komet-Penman MultiLingual; (Bateman, 1997)) system. One potential advantage of KPML over other generation systems and over many parsing systems is its multi-stratal design. The kinds of linguistic information included in KPML range from formal-syntactic (PoS, phrase structure) to functional-syntactic (syntactic functions), semantic (semantic roles/frames) and discoursal (e.g., theme-rheme, given-new). Also, since KPML has been applied to generate texts from a broad spectrum of domains, its lexicogrammatical resources cover a wide variety of registers—another potential advantage in the analysis of unrestricted text.

As well as our general concern with investigating the possible benefits of applying generation resources to the corpus annotation task, we are also more specifically concerned with a series of experiments involving the KPML system as such. Here, for example, we are working towards the construction of "treebanks" based on the theory of Systemic-Functional Linguistics (SFL; (Halliday, 2004)), so as to be able to empirically test some of SFL's hypotheses concerning patterns of instantiation of the linguistic system in authentic texts. Annotating the variety of linguistic categories given in SFL manually is very labor-intensive and an automated approach is clearly called for. We are also working towards a more detailed comparison of the coverage of the lexicogrammatical resources of KPML with those of parsing systems that are similarly theoretically-dedicated (e.g., the HPSG-based English Resource Grammar (ERG) (Copestake and Flickinger, 2002) contained in LinGO (Oepen et al., 2002)). Thus, the idea presented here is also motivated by the need to provide a basis for comparing grammar coverage across parsing and generation systems more generally.

The remainder of the paper is organized as follows. First, we present the main features of the KPML system (Section 2). Second, we describe the steps involved in annotation by generation, from the generation output (KPML internal generation record) to an XML representation and its refinement to an XML multi-layer representation (Section 3). Section 4 concludes the paper with a critical assessment of the proposed approach and a discussion of the prospects for application in the construction of corpora comparable in size and quality to existing treebanks (such as, for example, the Penn Treebank for English (Marcus et al., 1993) or the TIGER Treebank for German (Brants et al., 2002)). Since our description here has the status of a progress report of work still in its beginning stages, we cannot yet provide the results of detailed evaluation. In the final section, therefore, we emphasize the concrete steps that we are currently taking in order to be able carry out the detailed evaluations necessary.

2 Natural language generation with KPML

The KPML system is a mature grammar development environment for supporting large-scale grammar engineering work for natural language generation using multilingual systemic-functional grammars (Bateman et al., 2005). Grammars within this framework consist of large lattices of grammatical features, each of which brings constraints on syntactic structure. The features are also linked back to semantic configurations so that they can be selected appropriately when given a semantic specification as input. The result of generating with a systemic-functional grammar with KPML is then a rich feature-based representation distributed across a relatively simple structural backbone. Each node of the syntactic representation corresponds to an element of structure and typically receives on the order of 50-100 linguistic features, called the *feature selection*. Since within systemic-functional grammars, it is the features of the feature selection that carry most of the descriptive load, we can see each feature selection as an exhaustive description of its associated syntactic constituent. Generation within KPML normally proceeds on the basis of a semantic input specification which triggers particular feature selections from the grammar via a mediating linguistic ontology.

The features captured in a systemic-functional generation resource are drawn from the four components of functional meaning postulated within systemic-functional grammar: the ideational, expressing content-related decisions, the logical, expressing logical dependencies, the interpersonal, expressing interactional, evaluative and speech act information, and the textual, expressing how each element contributes to an unfolding text. It is in this extremely rich combination of features that we see significant value in exploring the re-use of such grammars for annotation purposes and corpus enrichment.

For annotation purposes, we employ some of the alternative modes of generation that are provided by the full grammar development environment—it is precisely these that allow for ready incorporation and application within the corpus annotation task. One of the simplest ways in which generation can be achieved during grammar development, for example, is by directly selecting linguistic features from the grammar. This can therefore mimic directly the task of annotation: if we consider a target sentence (or other linguistic unit) to be annotated, then selecting the necessary features to generate that unit is equivalent to annotating that unit in a corpus with respect to a very extensive set of corpus annotation features.

Several additional benefits immediately acrue from the use of a generator for this task. First, the generator *actually constructs the sentence* (or other unit) as determined by the feature selection. This means that it is possible to obtain immediate feedback concerning the correctness and completeness of the annotation choices with respect to the target. A non-matching structure can be generated if: (a) an inappropriate linguistic feature has been selected, (b) the linguistic resources do not cover the target to be annotated, or (c) a combination of these. In order to minimise the influence of (b), we only work with large-scale grammatical resources whose coverage is potentially sufficient to cover most of the target corpus. Further corpus instances that lie beyond the capabilities of the generation grammar used are an obvious source of requirements for extensions to that grammar.

Second, the architecture of the KPML system also allows for other kinds of annotation support. During grammar development it is often required that guidance is given directly to the semantics-grammar linking mappings: this is achieved by providing particular 'answers' to pre-defined 'inquiries'. This allows for a significantly more abstract and 'intention'-near interaction with the grammatical resource that can be more readily comprehensible to a user than the details of the grammatical features. This option is therefore also available for annotation.

Moreover, the semantic specifications used rely on a specified linguistic ontology that defines particular semantic types. These types can also be used directly in order to constrain whole collections of grammatical features. Providing this kind of guidance during annotation can also, on the one hand, simplify the process of annotation while, on the other, produce a semantic level of annotation for the corpus.

In the following sections, we see a selection of these layers of information working in annotation in more detail, showing that the kinds of information produced during generation corresponds extremely closely to the kinds of rich annotations currently being targetted for sophisticated corpus presentation.

3 Creating corpus annotations from KPML output

3.1 KPML output

The output produced by KPML when being used for generation is a recursive structure with the chosen lexical items at the leaves. Figure 1 shows the output tree for the sample sentence "However they will step up their presence in the next year".

The nodes of this structure may be freely annotated by the user or application system to contain further information: e.g., for passing through hyperlinks and URLs directly with the semantics when generating hypertext. Most users simply see the result of flattening this structure into a string: the generated sentence or utterance.

This result retains only a fraction of the in-

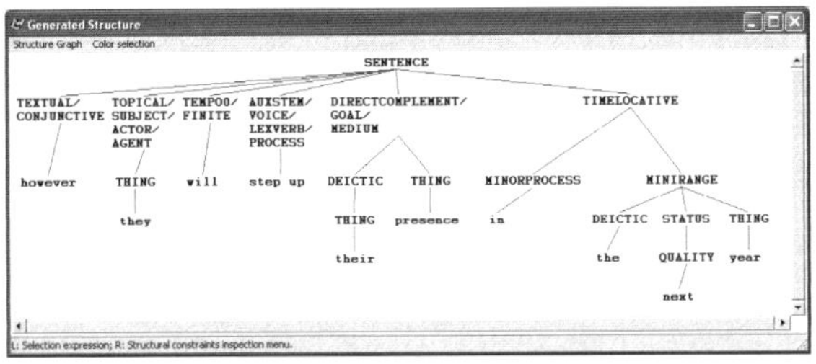

Figure 1: Tree generated by KPML

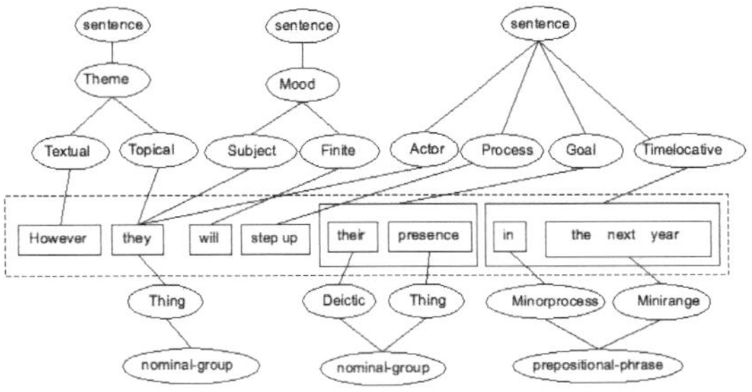

Figure 2: Generation output viewed as multi-layer annotation

```
<sfglayer metafunction="IDEATIONAL">
  However,
  &lt;segment functions="AGENT"&gt;they&lt;/segment&gt;
  will step up
  &lt;segment functions="DIRECTCOMPLEMENT GOAL MEDIUM"&gt;
    their presence
  &lt;/segment&gt;
  &lt;segment functions="TIMELOCATIVE"&gt;
    in the next year
  &lt;/segment&gt;

</sfglayer>
```

Figure 3: Metafunction+Function layers

formation that is employed by the generator during generation. Therefore, since we are using the grammar development environment rather than simply the generator component, we also have the possibility of working directly with the internal structures that KPML employs for display and debugging of resources during development. These internal structures contain a complete record of the information provided to the generation process and the generator decisions (including which grammatical features have been selected) that have been made during the construction of each unit. This internal record structure is again a recursive structure corresponding directly to the syntactic structure of the generated result and with each node having the information slots:

```
constituent:
{identifier,  \\ unique id for the unit
 concept,     \\ link to the semantic concept expressed
 spelling,    \\ the substring for this portion of structure
 gloss,       \\ a label for use in inter-lineal glosses
 features,    \\ the set of grammatical features for this unit
 lexeme,      \\ the lexeme chosen to cover this unit (if any)
 annotation,  \\ user-specified information
 functions    \\ the grammatical functions the unit expresses
}
```

An extract from such an internal record structure encoded in XML is given in the Appendix (5.1).

To support annotation, we make use of the XML-export capabilities of KPML (cf. (Bateman and Hartley, 2000)) in order to provide these completed structures in a form suitable for passing on to the next stage of corpus annotation within an XML-based multi-layer framework.

3.2 XML multi-layer representation

Systemic-functional analysis is inherently multidimensional in that SFL adopts more than one view on a linguistic unit. Here, we focus on three annotationally relevant dimensions: axis (features and functions), unit (clause, group/phrase, word, morpheme) and metafunction (ideational, logical, interpersonal and textual). Each metafunction may chunk up a given string (e.g., a clause unit) in different ways, thus potentially creating overlapping hierarchies. This is depicted schematically for the running example in Figure 2. For instance, in this example, according to the textual metafunction, "however they" constitutes a segment (Theme) and according to the interpersonal metafunction, "they will" constitutes another segment (Mood).

In order to be able to use the KPML output for annotation purposes, we adopt a multi-layer model that allows the representation of these different descriptional dimensions as separate layers superimposed on a given string (cf. (Teich et al., 2005)). The transformation from the KPML output to the concrete multi-layer model adopted is defined in XSLT.

From the KPML internal record structure we use the information slots of identifier, spelling, features, and functions. Each entry in the function slot is associated with one metafunctional aspect. For each metafunctional aspect, an annotation layer is created for each constituent unit (e.g., a clause) holding all associated functions together with the substrings they describe (see Figure 3 for the ideational functions contained in the clause in the running example).

An additional layer holds the complete constituent structure of the clause (cf. Figure 4 for the corresponding extract from the running example),

```
<constituent unit="-TOP-"
  selexp="LEXICAL-VERB-TERM-RESOLUTION...">
  <token features="HOWEVER">However,</token>
  <constituent unit="TOPICAL"
    selexp="THEY-PRONOUN...">
    <token features="THEY PLURAL-FORM">they</token>
  </constituent>
  <token features="OUTCLASSIFY-REDUCED...">will</token>
  <token features="DO-VERB...">step up</token>
  <constituent  unit="DIRECTCOMPLEMENT"
    selexp="NOMINAL-TERM-RESOLUTION OBLIQUE...">
    <constituent unit="DEICTIC"
      selexp="THEIR GENITIVE NONSUPERLATIVE...">
      <token features="THEIR PLURAL-FORM">their</token>
    </constituent>
    <token features="...COMMON-NOUN...">presence</token>
  </constituent>
  <constituent unit="TIMELOCATIVE"
    selexp="IN STRONG-INCLUSIVE UNORDERED...">
    <token features="IN">in</token>
    <constituent unit="MINIRANGE"
      selexp="NOMINAL-TERM-RESOLUTION...">
      <token features="THE">the</token>
      <constituent unit="STATUS"
        selexp="QUALITY-TERM-RESOLUTION...">
        <token features="...ADJECTIVE">next</token>
      </constituent>
      <token features="...COMMON-NOUN...">year .</token>
    </constituent>
  </constituent>
</constituent>
```

Figure 4: Constituent+Feature layer

i.e., the phrasal constituents and their features:

```
<constituent unit="..." selexp="...">
</constituent>
```

and the tokens and their (lexical) features:

```
<token features="..."> ... </token>
```

Thus, the KPML generation output, which directly reflects the trace of the generation process, is reorganized into a meaningful corpus representation. Information not relevant to annotation can be ignored without loss of information concerning the linguistic description. The resulting representation for the running example is shown in the Appendix (5.2).[2]

4 Discussion

Although it is clear that the kind of informational structures produced during generation with more developed KPML grammars align quite closely with that targetted by sophisticated corpus annotation, there are several issues that need to be addressed in order to turn this process into a practical annotation alternative. Those which we are currently investigating centre around usability and coverage.

[2]To improve readability, we provide the integrated representation rather than the stand-off representation which aligns the different layers by using character offsets.

Usability/effort. Users need to be trained in providing information to guide the generation process. This guidance is either in the form of direct selections of grammatical features, in which case the user needs to know when the features apply, or in the form of semantic specifications, in which case the user needs information concerning the appropriate semantic classification according to the constructs of the linguistic ontology. One of the methods by which the problem of knowing the import of grammatical features may be alleviated is to link each feature with sets of already annotated/generated corpus examples. Thus, if a user is unsure concerning a feature, she can call for examples to be displayed in which the particular linguistic unit carrying the feature is highlighted. Even more useful is a further option which shows not only examples containing the feature, but *contrasting* examples showing where the feature has applied and where it has not. This provides users with online training during the use of the system for annotation. The mechanisms for showing examples and contrasting sets of generated sentences for each feature were originally provided as part of a teaching aid built on top of KPML: this allows students to explore a grammar by means of the effects that each set of contrasting features brings for generated structures. For complex grammars this appears to offer a viable alternative to precise documentation—especially for less skilled users.

Coverage. When features have been selected, it may still be the case that the correct target string has not been generated due to limited coverage of grammar and/or semantics. This is indicative of the need to extend the grammatical resources further. A further alternative that we are exploring is to allow users to specify the correspondence between the units generated and the actual target string more flexibly. This is covered by two cases: (i) that additional material is in the target string that was not generated, and (ii) that the surface order of constituents is not exactly that produced by the generator. In both cases we can refine the stand-off annotation so that the structural result of generation can be linked to the actual string. Thus manual correction consists of minor alignment statements between generated structure and string.

Certain other information that may not be available to the generator, such as lexical entries, can be constructed semi-automatically on-the-fly, again using the information produced in the generation process (i.e., by collecting the lexical classification features and adding lexemes containing those features). This method can be applied for all open word classes.

Next steps. In our future work, we will be carrying out an extensive annotation experiment with the prediction that annotation time is not higher than for interactive annotation from a parsing perspective. TIGER, for example, reports 10 minutes per sentence as an average annotation time. We expect an experienced KPML user to be significantly faster because the process of generation or feature selection explicitly leads the annotator through precisely those features that are relevant and possible given the connectivity of the feature lattice defined by the grammar. Annotation then proceeds first by selecting the features that apply and then by aligning the generated structure with the corpus instance: both potentially rather rapid stages. Also, we would expect to achieve similar coverage as reported by (Baldwin et al., 2004) for ERG when applied to a random 20,000 string sample of the BNC due to the coverage of the existing grammars.

The results of such investigations will be SFL-treebanks, analogous to such treebanks produced using dependency approaches, LFG, HPSG, etc. These treebanks will then support the subsequent learning of annotations for automatic processing.

Acknowledgment. This work was partially supported by *Hessischer Innovationsfond* of TU Darmstadt and PACE (Partners for the Advancement of Collaborative Engineering Education: www.pacepartners.org).

References

T. Baldwin, E. M. Bender, D. Flickinger, A. Kim, and S. Oepen. 2004. Road-testing the EnglishResource Grammar over the British National Corpus. In *Proceedings of the 4th International Conference on Language Resources and Evaluation (LREC) 2004*, Lisbon, Portugal.

J. A. Bateman and A. F. Hartley. 2000. Target suites for evaluating the coverage of text generators. In *Proceedings of the 3rd International Conference on Language Resources and Evaluation (LREC)*, Athens, Greece.

J. A. Bateman, I. Kruijff-Korbayová, and G.-J. Kruijff. 2005. Multilingual resource sharing across both related and unrelated languages: An implemented, open-source framework for practical natural language generation. *Research on Language and Computation*, 3(2):191–219.

J. A. Bateman. 1997. Enabling technology for multilingual natural language generation: the KPML development environment. *Journal of Natural Language Engineering*, 3(1):15–55.

S. Bird and M. Liberman. 2001. A formal framework for linguistic annotation. *Speech Communication*, 33(1-2):23–60.

S. Brants, S. Dipper, S. Hansen, W. Lezius, and G. Smith. 2002. The TIGER treebank. In *Proceedings of the Workshop on Treebanks and Linguistic Theories*, Sozopol.

A. Cahill, M. McCarthy, J. van Genabith, and A. Way. 2002. Automatic annotation of the Penn-Treebank with LFG f-structure information. In *Proceedings of the 3rd International Conference on Language Resources and Evaluation (LREC) 2002*, Las Palmas, Spain.

A. Copestake and D. Flickinger. 2002. An open-source grammar development environment and broad coverage English grammar using HPSG. In *Proceedings of the 2nd International Conference on Language Resources and Evaluation (LREC)*, Athens, Greece.

A. Frank, L. Sadler, J. van Genabith, and A. Way. 2003. From treebank resources to LFG f-structures. Automatic f-structure annotation of treebank trees and CFGs extracted from treebanks. In A. Abeille, editor, *Treebanks. Building and using syntactically annotated corpora*, pages 367–389. Kluwer Academic Publishers, Dordrecht, Boston, London.

MAK Halliday. 2004. *Introduction to Functional Grammar*. Arnold, London.

M. P. Marcus, B. Santorini, and M. A. Marcinkiewicz. 1993. Building a large annotated corpus of English: the Penn Treebank. *Computational Linguistics*, 19(2):313–330.

S. Oepen, E. Callahan, D. Flickinger, C. D. Manning, and K. Toutanova. 2002. LinGO Redwoods. A rich and dynamic treebank for HPSG. In *Workshop on Parser Evaluation, 3rd International Conference on Language Resources and Evaluation (LREC)*, Las Palmas, Spain.

C.M. Sperberg-McQueen and C. Huitfeldt. 2001. GODDAG: A Data Structure for Overlapping Hierarchies. In *Proceedings of PODDP'00 and DDEP'00*, New York.

E. Teich, S. Hansen, and P. Fankhauser. 2001. Representing and querying multi-layer corpora. In *Proceedings of the IRCS Workshop on Linguistic Databases*, University of Pennsylvania, Philadelphia.

E. Teich, P. Fankhauser, R. Eckart, S. Bartsch, and M. Holtz. 2005. Representing SFL-annotated corpus resources. In *Proceedings of the 1st Computational Systemic Functional Workshop*, Sydney, Australia.

5 Appendix

5.1 Extract from generation record (clause level)

```
<example>
 <name>REUTERS29</name>
  <generatedForm>However, they will step up their presence in the next year.</generatedForm>
  <targetForm>But they will step up their presence in the next year.</targetForm>
  <structures><constituent id="G3324" semantics="STEP-3278">
   <functions>
     <function metafunction="UNKNOWN">SENTENCE</function></functions>
   <features/>
  <subconstituents><constituent id="G3308" semantics="RR62-3289">
   <functions>
     <function metafunction="TEXTUAL">TEXTUAL</function>
     <function metafunction="TEXTUAL">CONJUNCTIVE</function></functions>
   <features>
      <f>HOWEVER</f></features>
  <subconstituents><string>However,</string></subconstituents>
  </constituent><constituent id="G3310" semantics="PERSON-3291">
   <functions>
     <function metafunction="TEXTUAL">TOPICAL</function>
     <function metafunction="INTERPERSONAL">SUBJECT</function>
     <function metafunction="UNIFYING">ACTOR</function>
     <function metafunction="IDEATIONAL">AGENT</function></functions>
   <features/>
  <subconstituents><constituent id="G3309" semantics="PERSON-3291">
   <functions>
     <function metafunction="LOGICAL">THING</function></functions>
   <features>
      <f>THEY</f>
      <f>PLURAL-FORM</f></features>
  <subconstituents><string>they </string></subconstituents>
  </constituent>
  </subconstituents>
  </constituent><constituent id="G3311" semantics="ST59-3280-3297-3302">
   <functions>
     <function metafunction="LOGICAL">TEMPO0</function>
     <function metafunction="INTERPERSONAL">FINITE</function></functions>
   <features>
      <f>OUTCLASSIFY-REDUCED</f>
      <f>OUTCLASSIFY-NEGATIVE-AUX</f>
      <f>FUTURE-AUX</f>
      <f>PLURAL-FORM</f>
      <f>THIRDPERSON-FORM</f></features>
  <subconstituents><string>will </string></subconstituents>
  </constituent><constituent id="G3312" semantics="STEP-3278">
   <functions>
     <function metafunction="UNIFYING">AUXSTEM</function>
     <function metafunction="LOGICAL">VOICE</function>
     <function metafunction="LOGICAL">LEXVERB</function>
     <function metafunction="LOGICAL">PROCESS</function></functions>
   <features>
      <f>DO-VERB</f>
      <f>EFFECTIVE-VERB</f>
      <f>DISPOSAL-VERB</f>
      <f>STEM</f></features>
  <subconstituents><string>step up </string></subconstituents>
  </constituent><constituent id="G3316" semantics="PRESENCE-3292-3306">
   <functions>
     <function metafunction="IDEATIONAL">DIRECTCOMPLEMENT</function>
     <function metafunction="IDEATIONAL">GOAL</function>
     <function metafunction="IDEATIONAL">MEDIUM</function></functions>
  </constituent></subconstituents></constituent></structures>
  <selectionexpressions>
     <selexp sem="STEP-3278"><unit>-TOP-</unit><f>LEXICAL-VERB-TERM-RESOLUTION</f>
      <f>DO-NEEDING-VERBS</f><f>AUXSTEM-VOICE</f><f>REAL</f><f>NON-MOTION-CLAUSE</f>
      <f>PLURAL-FINITE</f><f>PLURAL-SUBJECT</f><f>TOPICAL-INSERT</f> ...
     </selexp>
     <selexp>...</selexp>
      ...
  </selectionexpressions>
</example>
```

5.2 Multi-layer representation of generation record

Metafunction+Function layers

```
<sfglayer metafunction="UNKNOWN">
  &lt;segment functions="SENTENCE"&gt;
    However, they will step up their presence in the next year .
  &lt;/segment&gt;
</sfglayer>

<sfglayer metafunction="UNIFYING">
  However,
  &lt;segment functions="ACTOR"&gt;they&lt;/segment&gt;
  will
  &lt;segment functions="AUXSTEM"&gt;step up&lt;/segment&gt;
  their presence in the next year .
</sfglayer>

<sfglayer metafunction="TEXTUAL">
  &lt;segment functions="TEXTUAL CONJUNCTIVE"&gt;However,&lt;/segment&gt;
  &lt;segment functions="TOPICAL"&gt;they&lt;/segment&gt;
  will step up their presence in the next year .
</sfglayer>
```

<sfglayer metafunction="LOGICAL">
  However,
  <segment functions="THING">they</segment>
  <segment functions="TEMPO0">will</segment>
  <segment functions="VOICE LEXVERB PROCESS">step up</segment>
  <segment functions="THING">their</segment>
  <segment functions="THING">presence</segment>
  in the
  <segment functions="QUALITY">next</segment>
  <segment functions="THING">year .</segment>
</sfglayer>

<sfglayer metafunction="INTERPERSONAL">
  However,
  <segment functions="SUBJECT">they</segment>
  <segment functions="FINITE">will</segment>
  step up
  <segment functions="DEICTIC">their</segment>
  presence in
  <segment functions="DEICTIC">the</segment>
  next year .
</sfglayer>

<sfglayer metafunction="IDEATIONAL">
  However,
  <segment functions="AGENT">they</segment>
  will step up
  <segment functions="DIRECTCOMPLEMENT GOAL MEDIUM">
    their presence
  </segment>
  <segment functions="TIMELOCATIVE">
    <segment functions="MINORPROCESS">in</segment>
    <segment functions="MINIRANGE">
      the
      <segment functions="STATUS">next</segment>
      year .
    </segment>
  </segment>
</sfglayer>

Constituent+Feature layer

<constituent id="G3324" unit="-TOP-"
  selexp="LEXICAL-VERB-TERM-RESOLUTION DO-NEEDING-VERBS AUXSTEM-VOICE REAL NON-MOTION-CLAUSE TOPICAL-INSERT ...">
  <token features="HOWEVER">However,</token>
  <constituent id="G3310" unit="TOPICAL"
    selexp="THEY-PRONOUN NONDEMONSTRATIVE-SPECIFIC-PRONOUN NOMINATIVE NONSUPERLATIVE NONREPRESENTATION NONPARTITIVE ...">
    <constituent id="G3309" unit="TOPICAL">
      <token features="THEY PLURAL-FORM">they</token>
    </constituent>
  </constituent>
  <token
    features="OUTCLASSIFY-REDUCED OUTCLASSIFY-NEGATIVE-AUX FUTURE-AUX PLURAL-FORM THIRDPERSON-FORM">
    will
  </token>
  <constituent id="G3312" unit="-TOP-">
    <token features="DO-VERB EFFECTIVE-VERB DISPOSAL-VERB STEM">
      step up
    </token>
  </constituent>
  <constituent id="G3316" unit="DIRECTCOMPLEMENT"
    selexp="NOMINAL-TERM-RESOLUTION OBLIQUE NONSUPERLATIVE NONREPRESENTATION NONPARTITIVE NONQUANTIFIED NOMINAL-GROUP ...">
    <constituent id="G3314" unit="DEICTIC"
      selexp="THEIR GENITIVE NONSUPERLATIVE NONREPRESENTATION NONPARTITIVE NONQUANTIFIED NOMINAL-GROUP ...">
      <constituent id="G3313" unit="DEICTIC">
        <token features="THEIR PLURAL-FORM">their</token>
      </constituent>
    </constituent>
    <constituent id="G3315" unit="DIRECTCOMPLEMENT">
      <token
        features="OUTCLASSIFY-PROPERNOUN NOUN COMMON-NOUN COUNTABLE SINGULAR-FORM NOUN">
        presence
      </token>
    </constituent>
  </constituent>
  <constituent id="G3323" unit="TIMELOCATIVE"
    selexp="IN STRONG-INCLUSIVE UNORDERED TEMPORAL-PROCESS LOCATION-PROCESS SPATIO-TEMPORAL-PROCESS PREPOSITIONAL-PHRASE ...">
    <token features="IN">in</token>
    <constituent id="G3322" unit="MINIRANGE"
      selexp="NOMINAL-TERM-RESOLUTION OBLIQUE NONSUPERLATIVE NONREPRESENTATION NONPARTITIVE NONQUANTIFIED NOMINAL-GROUP ...">
      <token features="THE">the</token>
      <constituent id="G3320" unit="STATUS"
        selexp="QUALITY-TERM-RESOLUTION SIMPLEX-QUALITY NOTINTENSIFIED NONSCALABLE CONGRUENT-ADJECTIVAL-GROUP ...">
        <constituent id="G3319" unit="STATUS">
          <token features="OUTCLASSIFY-DEGREE-ADJ ADJ-NEUTRAL-FORM ADJECTIVE">
            next
          </token>
        </constituent>
      </constituent>
      <constituent id="G3321" unit="MINIRANGE">
        <token features="OUTCLASSIFY-PROPERNOUN NOUN COMMON-NOUN COUNTABLE SINGULAR-FORM NOUN">
          year .
        </token>
      </constituent>
    </constituent>
  </constituent>
</constituent>

Constructing an English Valency Lexicon*

Jiří Semecký, Silvie Cinková
Institute of Formal and Applied Linguistics Affiliation
Malostranské náměstí 25
CZ11800 Prague 1
Czech Republic
(semecky,cinkova)@ufal.mff.cuni.cz

Abstract

This paper presents the English valency lexicon EngValLex, built within the Functional Generative Description framework. The form of the lexicon, as well as the process of its semi-automatic creation is described. The lexicon describes valency for verbs and also includes links to other lexical sources, namely PropBank. Basic statistics about the lexicon are given.

The lexicon will be later used for annotation of the Wall Street Journal section of the Penn Treebank in Praguian formalisms.

1 Introduction

The creation of a valency lexicon of English verbs is part of the ongoing project of the Prague English Dependency Treebank (PEDT). PEDT is being built from the Penn Treebank - Wall Street Journal section by converting it into dependency trees and providing it with an additional deep-syntactic annotation layer, working within the linguistic framework of the Functional Generative Description (FGD)(Sgall et al., 1986).

The deep-syntactic annotation in terms of FGD pays special attention to valency. Under valency we understand the ability of lexemes (verbs, nouns, adjectives and some types of adverbs) to combine with other lexemes. Capturing of valency is profitable in Machine Translation, Information Extraction and Question Answering since it enables the machines to correctly recognize types of events and their participants even if they can be expressed by many different lexical items. A valency lexicon of verbs is inevitable for the project of the Prague English Dependency Treebank as a supporting tool for the deep-syntactic corpus annotation.

We are not aware of any lexical source from which such a lexicon could be automatically derived in the desired quality. Manual creation of gold-standard data for computational applications is yet very time-consuming and expensive. Having this in mind, we decided to adapt the already existing lexical source PropBank (M. Palmer and D. Gildea and P. Kingsbury, 2005) to FGD, making it comply with the structure of the original Czech valency lexicons VALLEX (Žabokrtský and Lopatková, 2004) and PDT-VALLEX (J. Hajič et al., 2003), which have been designed for the deep-syntactic annotation of the Czech FGD-based treebanks (The Prague Dependency Treebank 1.0 and 2.0) (J. Hajič et al., 2001; Hajič, 2005). Manual editing follows the automatic procedure. We are reporting on a work that is still ongoing (which is though nearing completion). Therefore this paper focuses on the general conception of the lexicon as well as on its technical solutions, while it cannot give a serious evaluation of the completed work yet.

The paper is structured as follows. In Section 2, we present current or previous related projects in more detail. In Section 3, we introduce the formal structure of the EngValLex lexicon. In Section 4, we describe how we semi-automatically created the lexicon and describe the annotation tool. Finally in Section 5, we state our outlooks for the future development and uses of the lexicon.

* The research reported in this paper has been partially supported by the grant of Grant Agency of the Czech Republic GA405/06/0589, the project of the Information Society No. 1ET101470416, and the grant of the Grant Agency of the Charles University No. 372/2005/A-INF/MFF.

Proceedings of the Workshop on Frontiers in Linguistically Annotated Corpora 2006, pages 94–97,
Sydney, July 2006.

2 Valency Lexicon Construction

2.1 FGD

The Functional Generative Description (FGD) (Sgall et al., 1986) is a dependency-based formal stratificational language description framework that goes back to the functional-structural Prague School. For more detail see (Panevová, 1980) and (Sgall et al., 1986). The theory of FGD has been implemented in the Prague Dependency Treebank project (Sgall et al., 1986; Hajič, 2005).

FGD captures valency in the underlying syntax (the so-called tectogrammatical language layer). It enables listing of complementations (syntactically dependent autosemantic lexemes) in a valency lexicon, regardless of their surface (morphosyntactic) forms, providing them with semantic labels (functors) instead. Implicitly, a complementation present in the tectogrammatical layer can either be directly rendered by the surface shape of the sentence, or it is omitted but can be inferred from the context or by common knowledge. A valency lexicon describes the valency behavior of a given lexeme (verb, noun, adjective or adverb) in the form of valency frames.

2.2 Valency within FGD

A valency frame in the strict sense consists of inner participants and obligatory free modifications (see e.g. (Panevová, 2002)). Free modifications are prototypically optional and do not belong to the valency frame in the strict sense though some frames require a free modification (e.g. direction in verbs of movement). Free modifications have semantic labels (there are some more than 40 in PDT) and they are distributed according to semantic judgments of the annotators. FGD introduces five inner participants. Unlike free modifications, inner participants cannot be repeated within one frame. They can be obligatory as well as optional (which is to be stated by the judgment on grammaticality of the given sentence and by the so-called dialogue test, (Panevová, 1974 75)). Both the obligatory and the optional inner participants belong to the valency frame in the strict sense. Like the free modifications, the inner participants have semantic labels according to the cognitive roles they typically enter: ACT (Actor), PAT (Patient), ADDR (Addressee), ORIG (Origin) and EFF (Effect). Syntactic criteria are used to identify the first two participants ACT and PAT ("shifting", see (Panevová, 1974 75)). The other inner participants are identified semantically; i.e. a verb with one inner participant will have ACT, a verb with two inner participants will have ACT and PAT regardless the semantics and a verb with three and more participants will get the label assigned by the semantic judgment.

2.3 The Prague Czech-English Dependency Treebank

In order to develop a state-of-the-art machine translation system we are aiming at a high-quality annotation of the Penn Treebank data in a formalism similar to the one developed for PDT. When building PEDT we can draw on the successfully accomplished Prague Czech-English Dependency Treebank 1.0 (J. Cuřín and M. Čmejrek and J. Havelka and J. Hajič and V. Kuboň and Z. Žabokrtský, 2004) (PCEDT).

PCEDT is a Czech-English parallel corpus, consisting of 21,600 sentences from the Wall Street Journal section of the Penn Treebank 3 corpus and their human translations to Czech. The Czech data was automatically morphologically analyzed and parsed by a statistical parser on the analytical (i.e. surface-syntax) layer. The Czech tectogrammatical layer was automatically generated from the analytical layer. The English analytical and tectogrammatical trees were derived automatically from the Penn Treebank phrasal trees.

2.4 The Prague English Dependency Treebank

The Prague English Dependency Treebank (PEDT) stands for the data from Wall Street Journal section of the Penn Treebank annotated in the PDT 2.0 shape. EngValLex is a supporting tool for the manual annotation of the tectogrammatical layer of PEDT.

3 Lexicon Structure

On the topmost level, EngValLex consists of **word** entries, which are characterized by lemmas. Verbs with a particle (e.g. *give up*) are treated as separate word entries.

Each word entry consists of a sequence of **frame** entries, which roughly correspond to individual senses of the word entry and contain the valency information.

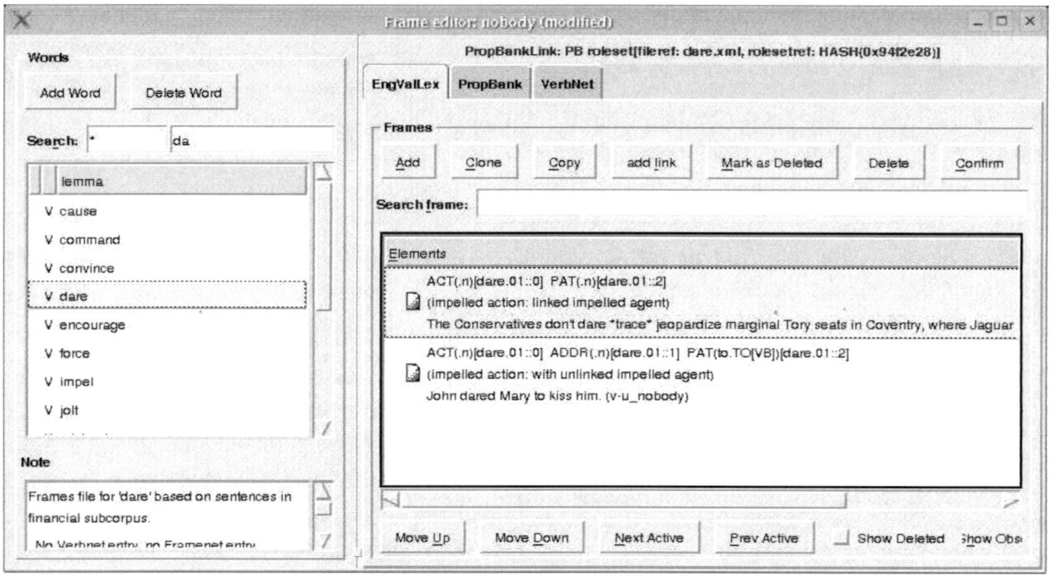

Figure 1: EngValLex editor: the list of words and frames

Each frame entry consists of a sequence of **valency slots**, a sequence of **example sentences** and a textual note. Each valency slot corresponds to a complementation of the verb and is described by a **tectogrammatical functor** defining the relation between the verb and the complementation, and a **form** defining the possible surface representations of the functor. Valency slots can be marked as optional, if not, they are considered to be obligatory.

The form is listed in round brackets following the functor name. Surface representations of functors are basically defined by combination of morphological tags and lemmas. Yet to save annotators' effort, we have introduced several abbreviations that substitute some regularly co-occurring sequences. E.g. the abbreviation **n** means '*noun in the subjective case*' and is defined as follows:

```
NN:NNS:NP:NPS
```

meaning one of the Penn Treebank part-of-speech tags: *NN*, *NNS*, *NP* and *NPS* (colon delimits variants). Abbreviation might be defined recursively.

Apart from describing only the daughter node of the given verb, the surface representation can describe an entire analytical subtree whose topmost node is the daughter of the given verb node. Square brackets are used to indicate descendant nodes. Square brackets allow nesting to indicate the dependency relations among the nodes of a given subtree. For example, the following statement describes a particle *to* whose daughter node is a verb.

```
to.TO[VB]
```

The following statement is an example of a definition of three valency slots and their corresponding forms:

```
ACT(.n)   PAT(to.TO[VB])
 LOC(at.IN)
```

The ACT (Actor) can be any noun in the subjective case (the abbreviation *n*), the PAT (Patient) can be a particle *to* with a daughter verb, and the LOC (Locative) can be the preposition *at*.

Moreover, EngValLex contains links to external data sources (e.g. lexicons) from words, frames, valency slots and example sentences.

The lexicon is stored in an XML format which is similar to the format of the PDT-VALLEX lexicon used in the Prague Dependency Treebank 2.0.

4 Creating the Lexicon

The lexicon was automatically generated from PropBank using XSLT templates. Each PropBank example was expanded in a single frame in the destination lexicon. When generating the lexicon, we have kept as many back links to PropBank as possible. Namely, we stored links from frames to Propbank rolesets, links from valency slots to PropBank arguments and links from examples to PropBank examples. Rolesets were identified by the roleset *id* attribute. Arguments were identified by the roleset *id*, the name and the function of the role. Examples were identified by the roleset *id* and their name.

After the automatic conversion, we had 8,215 frames for 3,806 words.

Tectogrammatical functors were assigned semi-automatically according to hand-written rules, which were conditioned by PropBank arguments. It was yet clear from the beginning that manual corrections would be necessary as the relations of Args to functors varied depending on linguistic decisions[1].

The annotators were provided with an annotation editor created on the base of the PDT-VALLEX editor. Apart from interface for editing EngValLex, the tool contains integrated viewers of PropBank and VerbNet, which allows offline browsing of the lexicons. Those viewers can be run as a stand-alone application as well and are published freely on the web[2]. The editor allows the annotator to create, delete, and modify word entries, and frame entries. Links to PropBank can be set up, if necessary.

Figure 1 displays the main window of the editor. The left part of the window shows list of words. The central part shows the list of the frames concerning the selected verb.

For the purpose of annotation, we divided the lexicon into 1,992 files according to the name of PropBank rolesets (attribute *name* of the XML element *roleset*), and the files are annotated separately. When the annotation is finished, the files will be merged again. Currently, we have about 80% of the lexicon annotated, which already contains the most difficult cases.

5 Outlook

We have annotated the major part of EngValLex. In the final version, a small part of the lexicon will be annotated by a second annotator in order to determine the inter-annotator agreement.

The annotation of the Prague English Dependency Treebank on the tectogrammatical level will be started soon and we will use EngValLex for assigning valency frames to verbs. The annotation will be based on the same theoretical background as the Prague Dependency Treebank.

Due to the PropBank links in EngValLex, we will be able to automatically derive frame annotation of PEDT from PropBank annotation of the Penn Treebank.

As the Wall Street Journal sentences are manually translated into Czech, we will be able to obtain their Czech tectogrammatical representations automatically using state-of-art parsers.

A solid platform for testing Czech-English and English-Czech machine translation will be given. In the future we will also try to improve the translation by mapping the Czech PDT-ValLex to the English EngValLex.

[1] E.g. Arg0 typically corresponds to ACT, and Arg1 to PAT when they co-occur. Yet, a roleset including an inchoative sentence (*The door.*ARG1 *opened.*) and a causative sentence (*John.*Arg0 *opened the door.*Arg1) will be split into two FGD frames. The causative frame will keep Arg0→ACT and Arg1→PAT whereas the inchoative will get Arg1→ACT.

[2] `http://ufal.mff.cuni.cz/~semecky/software/{propbank|verbnet}viewer/`

References

J. Hajič, 2005. *Complex Corpus Annotation: The Prague Dependency Treebank*, pages 54–73. Veda Bratislava, Slovakia.

J. Cuřín and M. Čmejrek and J. Havelka and J. Hajič and V. Kuboň and Z. Žabokrtský. 2004. Prague Czech-English Dependency Treebank Version 1.0. (LDC2004T25).

J. Hajič et al. 2001. Prague Dependency Treebank 1.0. LDC2001T10, ISBN: 1-58563-212-0.

J. Hajič et al. 2003. PDT-VALLEX: Creating a Large-coverage Valency Lexicon for Treebank Annotation. In *Proceedings of The Second Workshop on Treebanks and Linguistic Theories*, volume 9.

M. Palmer and D. Gildea and P. Kingsbury. 2005. The Proposition Bank: An Annotated Corpus of Semantic Roles. *Computational Linguistics*, 31(1):71.

J. Panevová. 1974–75. On verbal Frames in Functional Generative Description. *Prague Bulletin of Mathematical Linguistics (PBML)*, 22, pages 3–40, Part II, PBML 23, pages. 17–52.

J. Panevová. 1980. *Formy a funkce ve stavbě české věty [Forms and functions in the structure of the Czech sentence]*. Academia, Prague, Czech Rep.

J. Panevová. 2002. Sloveso: centrum věty; valence: centrální pojem syntaxe. In *Aktuálne otázky slovenskej syntaxe*, pages x1—x5.

P. Sgall, E. Hajičová, and J. Panevová. 1986. The Meaning of the Sentence in its Semantic and Pragmatic Aspects. *Academia, Prague, Czech Republic/Reidel Publishing Company, Netherlands.*

Z. Žabokrtský and M. Lopatková. 2004. Valency Frames of Czech Verbs in VALLEX 1.0. In *Frontiers in Corpus Annotation. Proceedings of the Workshop of the HLT/NAACL Conference*, pages 70–77, May 6, 2004.

Author Index